BEAM ME UP, SCOTTY™

BEAM ME UP, SCOTTY™

Star Trek®'s "Scotty"–
in his own words

JAMES DOOHAN
WITH PETER DAVID

POCKET BOOKS
New York   London   Toronto   Sydney   Tokyo   Singapore

Insert photos on pages 1, 2, 3, 4, 5, 6, 8, 10 and 16 (top) courtesy James Doohan; page 9 courtesy of Stephen Edward Poe (top), courtesy Greg Jein (bottom); pages 11, 12, 13, 14, 15 and 16 (bottom) courtesy of Paramount Pictures.

An *Original* Publication of POCKET BOOKS

POCKET BOOKS, a division of Simon & Schuster Inc.
1230 Avenue of the Americas, New York, NY 10020

Copyright © 1996 by James Doohan
All STAR TREK elements TM, ®, & © 1996 by Paramount Pictures.
All rights reserved. STAR TREK is a registered trademark of
Paramount Pictures. Used under authorization.

All rights reserved, including the right to reproduce
this book or portions thereof in any form whatsoever.
For information address Pocket Books, 1230 Avenue
of the Americas, New York, NY 10020

Doohan, James.
    Beam me up Scotty : Star Trek's "Scotty"—in his own words/
James Doohan with Peter David.
        p.   cm.
   ISBN 0-671-52056-3 (pbk)
    1. Doohan, James. 2. Star trek (Television program)
3. Television actors and actresses Canada Biography. I. David,
Peter (Peter Allen) II. Title.
PN2308.D66A3 1996
791.45'028'092—dc20   96-38340
[B]   CIP

First Pocket Books trade paperback printing December 1996

10 9 8 7 6 5 4 3 2 1

POCKET and colophon are registered trademarks of
Simon & Schuster Inc.

Cover design by Lisa Litwack

Printed in the U.S.A.

BEAM ME UP, SCOTTY™

Introduction

IN MY MIND'S EYE, I AM PICTURING A FAIRLY STOUTISH MAN, WITH a handsome face, silver gray hair, and a mustache that's shot through with gray, white, and black. When he does a movie, he has to dye it one consistent color, make some decisions on its behalf. Otherwise the white jumps from one side to the other as the hair grows in, going any old way it wants to. It's the kind of independently minded facial hair that would drive any film editor to distraction while trying to keep continuity from one scene to the next. Although, on the other hand, there's an entire base of fans who would probably love coming up with explanations for the changing colors, who are capable of producing entire treatises on the subject.

The stoutish man has bad legs, and the feet are worse than the legs. Their condition isn't helped by the fact that the man could stand to lose about twenty or more pounds. Give him credit: he's working on it. He gained the weight when he gave up smoking, which is a trade-off of sorts. So he tries not to eat what he used to, and his feet are certainly rooting for long-term success.

This gentleman is stepping through a shimmering dough-

1

nut-shaped portal on a faraway world, a portal that will graciously transport him back through time. For a moment, realities and possible realities shimmer around him.

There's one reality, for instance, in which he did not take a particular job on a particular TV series. He did not find himself typecast as a Scotsman and had a modestly successful career as a character actor.

There's another reality where he, in fact, became a widely respected thespian, renowned for his versatility and formidable acting range.

And then the world snaps into focus around him and he finds himself standing on the set of a newly up-and-running TV series called *Star Trek*. He stands there for a moment on the soundstage in Desilu Studios and spies a fortyish, slim actor reading the sides: the script pages for the day's shooting. The older man walks over to the younger, and the black-haired actor looks up, all unknowing, at his future self. At me.

"What's your name?" I ask.

"James Doohan," he says. He seems a bit shaky this day, and I know why. He inadvertently ran afoul of a sword-wielding cast mate, whose exuberant practice for an upcoming fencing scene almost resulted in young Doohan looking like one of those comedians with a trick blade or arrow through the head . . . except there would have been no trick to it. So young Doohan feels the need to stay particularly on his toes today.

"What part do you play?" I ask.

"I play the chief engineer."

"Do you do it as James Doohan?"

"No, no . . . I do it as a Scotsman." Clearly he's warming to the conversation.

"Why? Why do you do it as a Scotsman?"

And he proceeds to tell me energetically, and I pretend to listen. But, of course, I already know, and my thoughts are flashing farther back to my first meeting with Gene Roddenberry.

It is a time when *Star Trek* is not an icon, not a legend, not part of the fabric of society. Instead it's something almost unthinkable: a television show preparing to shoot a pilot (its second). In the future, fans will know the minutia of every episode and demand complete, consistent continuity from their *Star Trek*. Every last aspect of *Star Trek* will become, effectively, graven in stone.

But here is my first meeting with Gene Roddenberry, seated opposite me in his office at the Desilu Studios. Phone calls and visitors are being fielded in the reception area by Gene's secretary, one Dorothy C. Fontana. Gene is boisterous, loud, and enthusiastic, not yet weighed down by the heavy expectations bestowed upon him by the fans, some of whom will call him, only half-jokingly, Goddenberry.

Although Gene has a vision of the series as a whole, many pieces are yet to be fit together. He's very much open to input from a variety of sources.

He is asking me about the chief engineer of a space-going vessel called the *Enterprise*. Not telling me, you understand. *Asking* me. To be specific, he's asking me which of the eight different accents I've just done for him would best fit the role of the chief engineer.

"Well, if you want an engineer," I tell him, "it had better be a Scotsman, because in my experience Scotsmen are the best engineers I ever heard of. They've invented so many things, especially to do with ships. They've built enormous, fantastic bridges; the Firth of Forth is one of them. They've built all the great ships around the world—the *Queen Mary, Queen Elizabeth,* the *Titanic . . ."*

I am suddenly snapped out of my reverie by my younger self, repeating to me those words from my first meeting with Gene. I hear *"Titanic"* and look at young Doohan in a manner that says, *"Hmmm."*

Young Doohan, with mild chagrin, says defensively, "It did the wrong thing at the wrong time."

His admiration of the Scottish people is infectious. "Are you Scottish yourself?" I ask.

"I have some Scottish blood in me, but that's three hundred

years ago." He pauses, looking at me with curiosity. "Why are you asking all these questions?"

"Because I'm interested. What do you think is going to happen with your character?"

"I have no idea." He shrugs. "I just play the character, and I just have to do the best job I know how to do . . . and let the chips fall where they may after that."

I wonder how he would react if I told him. Would he be amused? Disbelieving? Horrified?

He wants only to be an actor, to play many different roles. He believes he has the ability to do just that, for he's been very well trained. Accents are just one of his acting tools, albeit one of his more useful. Even if he doesn't know an accent, all he has to do is hear it and alter the tone of his voice to duplicate it.

I quickly change the subject and ask him about his fellow cast members. What are his first impressions?

Well, over there is William Shatner, looking thoughtful—perhaps hatching another scheme to swipe Leonard Nimoy's bicycle. Young Doohan has worked with Bill Shatner before, way back in Toronto, in a one-hour TV drama on the Canadian Broadcasting Corporation called *The Well*. Doohan played a lawyer in charge of looking after Shatner, who in turn was playing a drunk—ostensibly the son of Stephen Butler Leacock (a noted professor at McGill University, expert in economics, history, and politics, not to mention a renowned and beloved humorist).

It's Doohan's impression that Bill operates more on instinct than anything else. He doesn't so much approach a character as leap on it and wrestle it to the ground; an outside-in approach rather than the other way around. It's a fly-by-the-seat-of-your-pants style of acting that's not really to Doohan's taste. Then again, it's said that an actor's real job is not so much acting as it is auditioning. Well, Bill excels at getting jobs, so judged on that basis he's extremely good at his profession.

Doohan points out another fellow on the set, running lines

4

for an upcoming scene. He has a serious, quiet demeanor and a pair of pointed ears that young Doohan considers to be not too well done. I'm tempted to assure him that in the future they will become very well done, very natural looking. Instead I simply nod my head and agree that the blend isn't very good. Even the most casual inspection reveals the line between the real ear and the fake.

Young Doohan murmurs, "Leonard Nimoy is supposed to be playing someone who's half human, half emotionless Vulcan. In his performance, though, he's playing more like ninety-five or ninety-eight percent of his character was the Vulcan, instead of fifty-fifty." I agree, but that observation notwithstanding, nobody can play Spock the way Leonard does; it's just fabulous.

George Takei, playing helmsman Sulu, is pointed out to me. "George is a pretty good actor," young Doohan says approvingly. "Playing a character who's Asian and being Asian, he doesn't exactly have to play against type. Basically, he plays himself. It would be interesting if he played a different character, one a little further from himself. But obviously George was hired because of his particular charm and demeanor. The thought seems to be that Sulu should be as close to George as possible because basically George was hired to be himself. That's that."

There's a mild stir, a snide comment here and there, originating from the crew and prompted by the fact that a certain late-arriving young actress has kept the crew waiting . . . again. Young Doohan inclines his head in the direction of latecomer Nichelle Nichols. "She does that occasionally," says young Doohan. I bite my tongue so as not to inform him that she will continue to do so, because Nichelle likes to play the star a lot. It usually takes her ten to twelve minutes to get onto the set after being called, and even Gene Roddenberry will scold her about that.

Unfortunately, Nichelle doesn't get too many opportunities to show what she can do, other than be very pretty, with a heck of a figure and gorgeous legs.

In the future I'll be waiting for her at conventions, and she'll find that the waiting game doesn't work with me. There will be times when a limo is scheduled to pick us up at a hotel to go to interviews and such. I'll tell her, "If you're not there on time, I'll take the limo. If you want to take a taxi, that's up to you. I won't hang around and wait fifteen or twenty minutes for you." After being left behind a couple of times, the *Enterprise* communication officer will get the message, and be much more punctual.

I stand next to the young Doohan, watching Nichelle, and am nonetheless reminded that all such trivialities are really just that: Trivial. We really love each other. She's a great gal, the kind that you just can't help but get to love the longer you know her.

Keeping to himself on the set is DeForest Kelley. "He might look familiar to you," says young Doohan. "He played the bad guy in westerns just about all the time. But here he's playing a terrific and sensitive doctor. It's an awfully good character. I like the way he and Spock banter with each other. No one could have played it better.

"That's Gene Roddenberry," continues young Doohan, unaware that in the future he and Gene will become good friends. They'll spend time together, shoot pool together, get lost at sea together. Lowering his voice, young Doohan says, "He tried to drop me from the show, until my agent got ahold of him. Don't know what my agent said to him; all I know is that, for the time being, I've got a job."

I can't resist it any longer. "It's going to be a lot longer than 'for the time being,' laddie," and I speak in an Aberdeen brogue. "It'll be forever."

He looks at me in utter confusion. "Who *are* you?" he asks, although I suspect he already knows.

And I know what I want to say. I want to say:

In the beginning, the fans would come up to me in the street and say, "Where's the accent?" And I would say, "Ach, ah only do that when ah get paid fer it. Now ye owe me fifty bucks."

In that respect, the thing is just one great big love affair. I have had "Beam me up, Scotty," hollered to me from across four lanes of freeway at seventy miles an hour. I've had cars come over close, with me in the fast lane. One BMW with four young businessmen in it caught up and one said, "Scotty, how you doin'?" Then they drove away, and I could tell that this was the most thrilling thing for those guys that day.

There was a car from out of town going along the Santa Monica freeway with a sticker that said, *Beam me up, Scotty, there's no intelligent life here.* As they pulled over to use the exit lane, I went by and waved, "Hi, fellas!" Their expression was worth the extra effort.

I remember once pulling alongside this big seven-passenger car. It could have been a Rolls-Royce or a Bentley. I wanted to warn the driver that it looked as if he was having problems with his front wheels. It wasn't until I had pulled alongside, in the midst of my intended good deed, that I realized the driver was Elvis Presley. So I called over to "The King," "You gotta get this to the garage; the front wheel shouldn't be doing that." And Elvis said, "Okay, Scotty."

No doubt about it. It's a great pleasure being Scotty. But there's the other side of the double-edged sword (a claymore, most likely), the side that's sliced away all the acting parts I've missed.

Typecasting is nothing new, of course. As you get more and more into the business, you realize that. The casting agents truly believe that audiences won't understand that actors can do different types of roles. And perhaps there's even some validity to the agents' belief. Cast members' doing other roles is accepted by *Star Trek* fans, but you have to be really into *Star Trek* to want to see James Doohan doing a different type of role. The others, non–*Star Trek* fans, don't want to see that; they want to see you being the same as you always are.

All this occurs to me, but then I look at the young Doohan—still so early in his career—and I think to myself, *Perhaps this is one of those alternate realities. Maybe in this reality, it will turn out differently for him. Why get into it with him?*

Why indeed?

"I'm just a fan," I say, and walk quickly away.

And that's not entirely true, I suppose. I certainly feel a strong connection with the fans. We've always had a pretty solid relationship, I like to think. I speak openly to them; I don't shade it. I don't color it with anything else. I just speak the basic truth as I see it.

In the more than two decades that I've been doing conventions, the fans have asked many, many questions of me. My ideal plan is to continue answering them forever. But every good miracle worker has to have a backup plan. Even Scotty, after all, couldn't change the laws of physics.

So this book you hold is my backup plan. A life well lived, I like to think. A voyage of discovery, which is certainly what *Star Trek* has always been about. I'll try to take you with me as best I can, from the emotional wounds of my difficult home life in Canada to the physical wounds sustained while storming the beach at Normandy. From the improbable beginning of my acting career through to my involvement with *Star Trek,* and beyond. All the positives and negatives that I owe to that television series that was considered a flop at the time and went on to become a part of our culture, while other TV shows considered hits at the time have vanished and been forgotten.

It's all here, as best as I can remember it. Not that I can remember it all, you understand. Much of it was a long time ago, and, as the saying goes, I didn't know at the time that there was going to be a quiz. So you'll forgive an old Aberdeen pub crawler the occasional lapse. After all, I'm not *really* a miracle worker.

I only play one on TV . . .

1

Birth of a Notion

MONTGOMERY SCOTT WAS BORN THREE TIMES.

The third time was in the office of Gene Roddenberry, as I mentioned earlier. Although Gene knew that he wanted a chief engineer, I had tremendous input into shaping Scotty's most notable traits.

The first time was in the nineteenth century.

Actually, that's not quite right. That's when his namesake was born, James Montgomery, my grandfather, for whom I named him. (So just in case you're under the impression that the "Montgomery" originated from the middle name of James Montgomery Doohan, now you know better.)

He had quite a life, my grandfather did, and lived to a very old age. I have an enormous picture of him, about four by four and a half feet, which was painted in Antwerp in 1853. People look at the year it was produced and assume he's my great-grandfather.

I thought it was rather apt to name Scotty for Montgomery, since the both of them had a taste for exploration in mighty sailing vessels. Of course, space was a bit out of reach for the original Montgomery. He set out to sea when he was sixteen and worked his way up to second mate.

A good thing he didn't achieve a higher rank faster than he did, because it might have cost him his life. For one voyage through the Indian Ocean turned into mutiny, resulting in the death of both the captain and the first mate. Montgomery quelled the mutiny, brought the ship home to Liverpool, and was given his master's certificate—a piece of paper certifying that he could captain a boat (which he was given on his next time out). Considering that Indian Ocean voyage, he'd certainly earned it. In fact, I still have the master's certificate, which gives me an idea of his age at the time of my mother's birth—seventy.

Yes, you read that right. Seventy.

Then again, he certainly had a lot of practice producing children. He had two wives and, God bless those sturdy women, *twenty-five children* between them—thirteen children by the first wife, twelve by the second. Most of the stress of child-rearing was left to his wives, considering he'd be gone six months at a time.

Finally, in order to accommodate his second wife, my grandmother, he bought her a pub in Ireland. From that point on, the children either worked at the pub or pursued other livelihoods.

My mother, Sarah Frances Montgomery, was one of the ones who didn't work in the pub. Sarah—called "Cissy" by everyone—grew into a beautiful, beautiful woman, with a well-proportioned face, a great nose and eyes (dark brown, good-sized eyebrows, not overdone or anything) and jet black hair. When she really got dressed up, she'd wear her hair all curled under. If you looked carefully, you could just make out the bottoms of her ears.

Sarah was a very religious woman; however, she decided to search out the religion she wanted. She started out a Presbyterian. She also went to the Salvation Army at one time, before deciding it wasn't really for her. Then she started going to Catholic churches, and she discovered that she wanted to know more. Eventually she decided that that was the church for her. That's *probably* where she met my father, William Patrick Doohan.

And, brother, she had a hell of a job with him.

As did I. For that matter, as did we all.

To be honest, difficulties with my father colored much of my early life, and perhaps more of my later life than is comfortable for me to think about.

William Patrick Doohan was nearly six feet tall, very wiry, and very, very intelligent. In fact, his intelligence worked against him when he wanted to become a trooper in World War I. They wouldn't let him into the Irish militia (the militia being somewhat akin to the National Guard, an organized means of keeping citizens in readiness for possible combat) because he was considered too valuable on the civilian side. He was a pharmacist, a veterinarian, and a dentist. His interest in joining the militia was probably motivated by two things.

The first was the urge to escape from the life in which he was brought up. My paternal grandfather, Thomas Doohan, was the chief constable of Belfast up until 1917 and a very rigid disciplinarian, very strict with my father and his six siblings. As children, William and his younger brother, John, had to wash up outside the house, although their sisters could use the bathrooms inside. Imagine bathing outside in Belfast, in bitter, bitter cold water. It was possible to heat the water, but the air was still freezing during the frosty, six-month-long Belfast winter.

Plus, the situation in Belfast for Catholics was not a pleasant one. There was a little less of the anti-Catholic stuff while my father was growing up, but it was present nevertheless. The problem was that the British felt they had to keep the Irish under control. Three hundred years ago, the British had brought in Scottish settlers to the northern part of Ireland, hoping to control the Irish. But you can't control the

Irish. Consequently, both my father and his younger brother, John, had to take back roads to and from school. This didn't spare them from being beaten up quite a number of times.

So putting distance between himself, Belfast, and his father was his first priority—and one with which I would, ironically, be able to sympathize in later years.

What was the second thing that motivated him to want to join the militia? Regretfully, it was because they had a private club where he could have gone and gotten drunk.

Because my father, you see, was an alcoholic. Indeed, in later years when he got angry, bordering on violent, he would say sharply that he was going to "go out to the officers' mess."

Since his not being allowed to join the army meant that he couldn't escape physically, he used the drink to escape mentally. And he kept on doing it, as you'll see. He just couldn't handle his own life, whatever it was, and allowed the drink to handle his life instead.

My father held down several jobs, working at a large pharmacy called Tate's. Then he went to his own drugstore (called a "chemist's shop" over there) and would do dental work as well, plus he'd fix animals in the backyard or travel around the county fixing cows and horses and everything else. It was around that time that my father (around twenty-five years old at the time) and mother got married.

In short order, they had my two older brothers, William and Thomas, and my older sister, Margaret. At the point when my mother was pregnant with me, the general situation in Belfast was deteriorating. My parents decided that it was time to get out. It was a terrible place to bring up children. Credit my father with that, at least. He didn't want his own children to experience as miserable an upbringing as he himself had had. If only he could have left his drinking behind in Belfast, then his family's life might have reached the ideal situation he was trying for.

My parents were split on where to go. My father preferred South Africa, because that was the new country, but my mother wanted to go to Vancouver, British Columbia, in

Canada. Her sister Isabel—a small woman, about five one, whom we called Aunt Bell—lived there. Since I was *in utero* at the time, I wasn't exactly in on their conversations, but I know my mother convinced him that Canada was the place to go.

They landed in Halifax on New Year's Day 1920, and I was born March 3, 1920 (which would be, chronologically, the second birth of Montgomery Scott . . . for those keeping track). I tell people, when they ask, "I'm a good sailor and I love trains," because my parents then went by train 5,400 miles from Halifax right through to British Columbia.

While we lived in Vancouver, my mother exercised her seamstress skills. She was a seamstress like you wouldn't believe. She made all my brothers' clothes, my father's clothes—suits, vests, the whole thing. She used to make all my sister's clothes as well. She would have all the fashion catalogs and check them out to get patterns. As a child, I would play with the pedal of her Singer sewing machine. She'd say with that infinite patience and Irish lilt, "Okay, if you want to work the pedal, you just go ahead and work it," and I'd do it until she said it was enough.

Her work was so excellent, in fact, that it would draw comment. When I was grown, my sister came to visit me while I was acting in the Neighborhood Playhouse in New York City. One day we were standing at Tiffany's window, looking in, and I could see women come along and check the stitching of her clothes, muttering to themselves about it in appreciation.

My sister, Margaret, was about two and a half years older than I was. She was an Rh-factor child and was always weak, nor was she especially pretty, and I loved her dearly. In her later years, ill health would continue to plague her. She got tuberculosis when she was working at Imperial Oil and spent the next year in a hospital in London, Ontario. Her job cost her a lung.

Yet, after a year at the hospital's sanatorium, she went back to work at the oil company. They did everything they could to treat her as well as possible, which—for the time—was rather considerate. Hell, nowadays if the same thing had happened, she could very likely have filed a lawsuit against the company and gotten an extremely hefty settlement. Instead, she was happy enough that the company willingly accommodated her frailty, providing her with a cot where she could lie down anytime she wanted to.

As long as I'm talking about my siblings, I should discuss my older brothers as well—although it was I who suffered the brunt of my father's drinking difficulties, since they had their own lives that they were pursuing.

Tom was the eldest, eight years older than I. He was a lovely guy, although the age difference and his own activities kept us somewhat distant when we were kids. How many fourteen-year-olds hang out with their six-year-old kid brothers, after all? In recent years, family disputes added an emotional distance that's distressing for all concerned, and, unfortunately, Tom died last October 12, 1995. I had been planning to send him a copy of this book when it came out; perhaps somehow he'll still manage to see it.

My brother Bill, William Patrick Doohan, is six years older than I and was the smartest one in the family. He received top scores all across the board when he went to high school (unlike myself, who would do well in chemistry, physics, and math and get *C*s in everything else). Bill had a photographic memory, you see. He'd look at a page for five seconds, then turn it and remember the entire thing. He was a great guy, a good big brother . . . although, again, he really didn't have much to do with the tension that grew between my father and me.

My father spent most of his life just doing research, which resulted in our relocating to Sarnia, Ontario, when I was six. My father worked out of a laboratory there, and one of the things he was hoping to discover was a cheap way to separate oil from tar sands in the Mackenzie River Basin. There's a ton of oil there, but it's very difficult to separate. I'd love to be able to tell you that my father made a breakthrough, made a fortune, kicked the booze, and we all lived happily ever after. Unfortunately, although he made a living as a researcher, he never quite achieved that lofty goal. The tar sands continue to hold on jealously to their oil.

Sarnia is right across the river from Port Huron, Michigan, sixty miles from Detroit. The house I grew up in was gray, dormer-style, three bedrooms upstairs; one bathroom, and a fairly good-size hallway. My parents had one bedroom, my sister the second, and I shared the third with my brothers. I slept on a cot, while they slept in a big double bed. There was a large veranda all the way across the front. Most of the houses in that area were fairly close to each other, but there was a good-size driveway in between, though we didn't have a car for a good long time. My father didn't want to spend the money, and besides . . . he was afraid to drive because of his drinking.

We didn't have a car until my brothers Tom and Bill started to work. Tom was the first to work, bringing in seventeen dollars a week. He would keep two dollars and give the rest to my mother. My brother Bill would do the same thing.

In the meantime, my father was keeping half of his salary for drinking.

Being the youngest, I guess I was more easily affected by it. There I would be, aged eight or so, and my father would be downstairs and violently angry, infuriated by something that somebody had said or done. Then he would storm out and not come back until midnight or so, raging and drunk from having "visited the officers' mess." I would lie awake until he settled down, and then my brothers would come in at one o'clock or so in the morning. They were completely unaffected by him and his drinking, because they were teenage young men, out and about with their own concerns. Margaret, for her part, was simply too frail to be any sort of real ally. Whether it was genuinely the case or whether I'd built it up that way in my own mind, I nonetheless felt very small and very alone.

Yet my father was a study in contradictions, because

despite his drunkenness and his violence, he never struck my mother. He once horsewhipped me, though. He took it into his head that I'd stolen something from nearby a local church, and there, in the upstairs hallway, he started to whale me with a horsewhip.

I tried to cover up, duck my head away, ward off the blows, but I was only eight years old. There was only so much I could do, and there was nowhere to run as the horsewhip kept descending. "Willie, Willie, no!" my mother screamed, trying to get in between him and me. "That's enough, Willie, *that's enough!*" Finally her shrieks seemed to get through to him. Either that or he felt his point had been made, or perhaps he was just tired or bored or wanted to go out for another drink, but finally the beating ceased. My body was throbbing all over; any endeavor by my mother to touch me or hold me consolingly, to ease my sobs, would only have resulted in more pain.

I never felt more alone, more frustrated, and I was certain that my father saw me as nothing more than something to abuse.

And yet . . .

Diphtheria is practically unknown these days, since infants are routinely immunized against it. But when I was a child, it was an incredibly infectious and deadly disease. The illness starts with a fever, sore throat, and swollen glands. A thick white membrane forms on the tonsils, making it difficult to breathe. Standard treatment was with antitoxins and penicillin, although more advanced or dire cases could require a tracheotomy. Heart attacks were not uncommon, nor was death. Diphtheria was the dreaded killer of children.

And when I was eight, I contracted it.

I first came down with it while peforming my duties as an altar boy at St. Joseph's Church with Father McCarthy. It was a Sunday service. We stood there in our red cassocks with white lace surplice, and Father McCarthy was conducting one of his usual wonderful services.

And right there, in the middle of mass, I suddenly became

delirious. The churchgoers must have been wondering what had happened to me. Possession? Would I start speaking in tongues, perhaps with my head spinning around? But I'm sure that some of them realized the truth, and the truth was more frightening than any fanciful fiction they might spin. I was taken out immediately and brought to my home, where I was quarantined.

I lay there on my cot, sweating through the sheets and struggling to breathe. The family doctor, Dr. Rutherford, would come to treat me as I lay there suffering from delirium. My memories of the time, understandably, are something of a blur, an agglomeration of images: my mother's frightened face, the doctor looking down at me in concern, and the needles that he drove right into my stomach.

And my father?

My father, banned from the house because of the quarantine, would bring me toys and hand them to my mother at the back door.

Apparently there was something about my being ill that brought out the best in my father. Some years later, after World War II, I contracted pneumonia and was delirious again. I heard him say to my mother with great concern, "Cissy, I think we're gonna lose this boy."

How tragic, really, that it took near-fatal disease to bring out the parental concern in my father. In a way, though, he did lose me . . . but it was his personality, not any disease, that drove us apart.

But that would come later.

2

Planes, Trains, and Automobiles

IN RETROSPECT, THE ROLE OF THE *ENTERPRISE*'S CHIEF ENGINEER was a natural fit, because I was always really interested in things that "went," things that were in motion. The ideal thing for me would have been a bicycle, but my mother couldn't afford to buy me one. I would gladly have tried to earn it. Once I approached my father about wanting to sell newspapers. I saw no harm in it. After all, this was the Great Depression, and there were people out on the streets selling apples just to try to survive.

But my father didn't hesitate. "No," he said sharply, "you're not going to do that." He didn't feel he had to explain why, although I suppose the answer was rooted in false pride. It was the notion that "We Doohans don't do that sort of thing."

I was allowed to pursue my hobby of trains, however. Toy trains, of course (an appropriate enough hobby for a future "engineer," I imagine). One Christmas they gave me a windup train with an enormous amount of accessories. It was probably the biggest windup available at the time. I had three or four boxcars, a couple of flatcars, and it all looked fabulous. The key was on the right-hand side, and I'd sit there turning that key and watching the train cruise the tracks. I would lie there, putting my face right down on the carpet and watching the train come right at me. Some kids would be interested in building entire towns for the trains to run through, but not me. If it had been surrounded by nothing but bare grass, that would have been enough for me. I just loved the trains. Still do, in fact. Although I did have some unusual cargo that I'd have the trains pull—bullets. I would take my father's ammunition, .45 bullets, and I'd put them on the flatcars. Have the trains haul them around.

It might seem a little startling nowadays that, as a child, I played with live ammo, but that's what I did. My father was an expert shot, and he had a lot of guns, pistols, and assorted firearms. In retrospect, considering his general frustration with life and his alcoholism, it's probably a damned good thing he never started waving around one of his weapons while he was drunk. The guns exited the house, though, when the war came along in later years, because the Royal Canadian Mounted Police (RCMP) told him, "Willie, you have to turn your guns in." It wasn't for the war effort, but because they wanted to maintain internal security.

Also, when we'd have a good rain, I'd go and get a piece of wood, cut a notch out in the back, point the front like a ship, and make battleships. I'd put an elastic band on the back, wrap up a paddle, tighten it up, put it on the puddles, and let it go. All my battleships were paddle steamers.

It was also a time of tremendous advances in aviation. There was an excitement, a romanticism about it that would be hard for anyone who's grown up in the modern age to fully grasp. I was seven when, in 1927, Lucky Lindy (Charles Lindbergh) made his famed landing in Paris, and twelve when Amelia Earhart completed her acclaimed solo trip from Newfoundland to Ireland. (Earhart vanished five years later. General speculation was that she was a prisoner of the Japanese. Little did we suspect she'd been kidnapped by aliens, as *Voyager* eventually revealed . . .)

What an incredible, remarkable lure aviation was. For a young boy who felt trapped by his circumstances, the concept of climbing into a cockpit and just leaving everything behind . . . of escaping . . . was an incredibly attractive one. But when you're ten years old, such things are pipe dreams, nothing more than that.

As I mentioned earlier, we didn't have a car for quite some time. This didn't mean that I never got to ride around in one, however. One I remember in particular was a gorgeous, upper-priced car called a Hudson brougham, with wonderfully cushy seats. Then again, it's hard to forget a car that you almost get killed in.

The car belonged to my "Aunt" Kitty, who wasn't always in a position to own such a fine automobile. Once upon a time in Ireland, she was simply Kitty Brown, poor as a church mouse, and my mother used to help her and make dresses for her.

She moved to Cleveland and went to work as a secretary for a man named Frank Schneider, a big, boisterous German fellow who worked for a finance company owned by a Mr. Mackie. In the sort of relationship that seems far more fraught with peril in these days of sexual harassment charges, Kitty and Frank fell in love and eventually married. Frank became by extension "Uncle" Frank, and their children (five in all, eventually) were my "cousins": the eldest, a boy named Frank, Jr., and four girls, Gwendolyn, Betsy, Bernadette, and Leslie.

In time, Mr. Mackie passed away, and since he had no relatives, he left the company to the Schneiders. After that, money was no longer a problem, particularly after Uncle Frank parlayed it into a franchise called the Household Finance Corporation of America (which you may have heard of). They had all the money in the world and the greatest cars: Packards, LaSalles, and similar vehicles.

Aunt Kitty and my mother just got along like a house afire. They obviously loved each other, and we were regular visitors at the Schneiders' home.

Uncle Frank was a terrific guy. Every now and then he

would blow his top because the girls had so many clothes and they never wore half of them. He'd get angry and cut off their allowance, which was a pretty considerable action because their allowance was *four hundred dollars a month.* "Pack up the clothes, and we're driving out to an orphanage!" he'd bellow. "And you're going to give these clothes away that you bought so foolishly."

Undaunted by income stoppage, the girls would show up at one of the offices and tell one of the managers, "We've been cut off. We want to work for you." They'd try to effect disguises just in case Uncle Frank should spot them, but they were really pathetic disguises—Rubber bands wrapped around their faces, that sort of thing. I'm sure Uncle Frank was *really* fooled by that clever maneuver.

I spent five or six weeks of the summer with them, and I did it for every other summer up until I was in my late teens. The Schneider family was a big part of my life, and I wish they'd get in touch with me now, because I've lost their addresses. (Betsy, Leslie, Gwendolyn, Bernadette [Barney, we used to call her], and Frank, Jr., please, if you read this book or even hear about it, I'd love to hear from you. I'm the same guy you knew years ago, long before I ever became an actor.)

When I was eleven, I was riding in Aunt Kitty's car, the aforementioned Hudson brougham. My brother Tom was driving, and my mother, Kitty, and I were passengers.

We were in Dearborn, Michigan, when the accident happened.

Everything seemed to be going fine, and then at an intersection, a car broke through a red light and hit the front on the driver's side, and as we slewed around, it plowed into the back end.

The moments after that were somewhat confusing to me. I was kind of dazed, and my brother Tom was walking with me. Then I spotted one of the passengers from the other car, just lying there on the ground, unmoving. He had, of all things, a wooden leg.

We were put into an ambulance that, instead of a siren, had

an extremely bizarre crank that sounded like a turkey being shoved through a meat grinder. The ambulance roared up and drove us toward the brand-new River Rouge Ford plant, because that was the location of the nearest emergency hospital.

They also wanted to see what they could do for the wooden-legged man, to see if they could revive him. As it turned out, they didn't have the opportunity; when I'd seen him lying there after the crash, he was already dead.

I was in the ambulance, sitting on Tom's knee. We were heading straight toward a train track crossing, and a lot of cars were stopped, waiting. The ambulance just tore right through the whole thing, dodging past the cars and hurtling across the track. All the times I'd lain on the floor, nose-to-nose with my toy train, and now here was the real thing bearing down on us, a massive engine with the whistle blasting, warning us off. But the ambulance driver knew he had time. I think there were thirty or forty yards to go before the train would have crossed the road. The tricky thing about such a maneuver is that it's very easy to misjudge the train's speed. You can think you have all the time in the world as you cut across the tracks, and then before you know it, the thing's right on top of you. Fortunately enough, this driver timed it right. "Wow!" I said wonderingly to him. "You can just go through anything!"

The hospital there was all brand-new, built around 1929. Once we were at the plant hospital, we got patched up. All things considered, we got off lucky. I had a small nick on my head and on my finger, a scar that I carry to this day. My mother and Aunt Kitty had similar cuts and bruises. They even managed to make the car drivable after all that.

My brother, however, didn't get off quite that easy. Oh, he was relatively uninjured, but they tossed him in jail overnight until they could determine who was responsible for the accident. After all, a man had died. To be honest, it wasn't exactly the most grueling jail stay that anyone ever had. They didn't lock his cell, and one of the police officers even brought him back to have dinner with us. Eventually matters were handled by Uncle Frank, who put up bail and then saw things through so that Tom was cleared of any possible wrongdoing.

We stayed at the Dearborn Inn, a very plush inn built by Henry Ford. He built it as a sort of defensive measure. He was tired of having guests show up and stay at his home, so he created the Dearborn Inn . . . and charged guests for staying there. Questionable hospitality, I suppose, but good business sense.

At one point I was sitting on the front steps of the inn, which were quite broad, about twenty-five or thirty feet. A skinny fellow with a fedora, nattily dressed in a dark gray suit and a string bow tie, dropped down onto the wide step next to me. He acted as if we'd been the best of friends for the longest time and started chatting with me about the accident. We talked for about fifteen minutes, and then he got up and left.

Immediately people started clustering around me. Naturally, I wondered what I had done wrong. And they were all whispering, "What'd he say? What'd he say?"

I looked around in confusion. "Wha—? Wha—?" I managed to stammer out. I couldn't figure it out. I'd been minding my own business, talking with some guy, and suddenly everyone was acting as if something amazing had just occurred.

"That was Henry Ford!" one of the people said, and others bobbed their head in agreement.

I've been a Ford man ever since.

3

That's Entertainment

"YOU KNOW, YOU CAN DO ANYTHING YOU WANT TO DO WITH US, Jimmy," said Lenore.

This is the sort of thing a girl, or girls, might say to me in my later years that would garner my extreme interest and enthusiasm.

However, in this particular case, I was eleven years old, and I wasn't sure what the hell Lenore (an older woman of thirteen) was talking about.

We were walking through a field of high grass, coming home after a party at school. It was just starting to get dark, with the first of the evening stars peeping into existence and a gentle breeze wafting across the field.

In addition to Lenore, there was another girl there, about my age, named Rita. And Lenore kept saying, "You know, you can do anything you want to do with us, Jimmy."

Now, it's not as if I knew *nothing*. Certainly I was a veteran of clandestine games of doctor between the ages of five and seven. (Well, what did you expect? That I got a young female playmate alone and said, "Want to play engineer?")

Nevertheless, Lenore was being *extremely* aggressive. This

called for me to be suave, in control, with a ready quip or the just-right-thing to say to her overtures.

I said, "Oh."

Well, she said it a couple more times, and I quickly got the feeling that "Oh" wasn't going to carry me too far. But I was uncomfortable with Rita standing close-by, so I said, "Well, will you send Rita over there?" Which she did.

It was my first sexual encounter—not "all the way," you understand, but it certainly brought playing doctor to an entirely new level. I don't know where Lenore learned the things she did to me that evening, although at the time the source was of much less importance to me than the deeds. Every nerve ending in my eleven-year-old body was screaming, *"What's going on down there?!?"* Especially when Lenore called Rita over and started giving her instructions as well . . .

Of course, for every action, there's an equal and opposite reaction. The reaction came when I got home. My mother frowned slightly because I was home an hour later than I'd said I would be. No doubt my slightly glazed look, broad smile, and somewhat erratic walk as I moved past cued her that something had been . . . you should pardon the expression . . . up. But let's face it, Sarah "Cissy" Doohan didn't exactly have to be Sherlock Holmes to figure out what had . . . again, pardon the expression . . . gone down, when she noticed the grass stains all over my back. I would have made an abysmal master criminal; hiding clues simply wasn't uppermost in my mind.

"What have you been *doing?!*" my mother exclaimed, although I strongly suspect she had a pretty good idea.

I craned my neck, noticed the incriminating grass stains, and figured the best way to cover a lie is to coat it with a half-truth. "We were . . . wrestling," I said.

She stared down at me, and then without another word, gestured that I should get upstairs. I have no idea if she said anything to my father. If she had, truthfully I'm not sure if he would have reacted with outrage or with a barely contained smirk.

Interestingly, I didn't hang out with those girls after that. You'd think I *would* . . . but I don't know if I was prepared for girls who were quite that aggressive. I don't know if I ever was, really.

It *was* 1931, after all. If one was seeking entertainment, one couldn't exactly plop down in front of a television. I didn't even *see* a television until the Great Lakes Exposition, held in Cleveland in the late 1930s. Accompanied by Aunt Kitty and my cousins, we saw a demonstration of a round-screened television. It was exciting to see this new invention, even though I had no idea to what uses it could be put. I was nonetheless amazed by it and wondered how long down the road it would be before it was in people's homes.

I wasn't a visionary, or anything like that. I lived too much in the present, concerned about such mundane things as having a few cents in my pocket, to worry about whether television would be (as many claimed) a passing fad. If someone had come to me from the future and told me I'd actually be spending a respectable portion of my life on that little screen, I wouldn't have known what to make of it. Then again, the future can be a strange place.

So television wasn't really a part of my growing up—an inconceivable idea nowadays, considering that television is so much a part of everyday life that when people complain about "inappropriate" material on television damaging their children, it never *occurs* to them that they don't *have* to own a television. People have stolen televisions at gunpoint, I'm sure, but I doubt that anyone ever put a gun to someone's head and said, "You *must* keep this thing in your house."

No, we had radio. Our first radio was shaped like a cathedral window, about fourteen inches tall. Then we got a big Rogers model, Rogers Sound and Music being a big Canadian manufacturer at the time. I'd sit in front of the radio, listening to things like baseball games. My mother, who never saw a ball game in her life, came to adore Ty Tyson, radio announcer for the Detroit Tigers. "He's just fascinating," she would sigh. She probably didn't listen to the substance of what he was saying. She just liked listening to his voice.

There were mystery shows: "Gather round and listen to . . . the Shadow!" I didn't listen to any science fiction radio shows (although I did thrill to the comic strip adventures of Buck Rogers in the *Detroit Free Press*). We used to listen to *Amos 'n' Andy* and then-famous singers such as Russ Columbo or Vaughn Monroe.

My favorite show was *Chandu the Magician.* Chandu would have his adventures in such exotic locales as Indonesia and Sumatra, and every episode was fraught with spooky moments and creepy Oriental-style music.

The sponsor was chocolate-coated Ex-Lax. They said on the radio that you could get a free sample just by sending in a postcard. Now, I didn't know what Ex-Lax was, but if it was chocolate coated, that was good enough for me. I sent away for it and got it, but my father intercepted it.

"Whose is this?" he demanded.

"Mine," I said nervously. I wondered what I could possibly have done wrong.

"Do you know what it is?" he said, waving it at me.

"No," I told him.

Although he was doubtlessly annoyed that I had sent for something without his permission, I think he might also have been ever-so-slightly amused by the situation. "It makes you go to the bathroom very fast!" he informed me.

This seemed a little odd to me. Why should anyone need a chocolate anything to go to the bathroom? And hastily, for that matter?

Perhaps I should have sent for secret decoder rings. At least those have high resale value these days. I don't think anyone would be interested in shelling out serious money for a sixty-year-old Ex-Lax tablet . . . unless someone were a *serious* fan of chocolate.

Hmm. Maybe I should give George Takei a call . . .

Her name was Kay Glynn.

I was about fifteen when I first noticed her. You know the type of moment. You look at a girl and suddenly that moment seems to pass between the two of you, that sort of Hey, where did *you* come from. As if you're "recognizing" someone for the first time. Some people believe in reincarnation, claiming that souls move in karmic circles and we keep encountering those we've known before. I've some modest interest in the psychic world, but I'm not sure I buy into it that far.

But I do know that one day I looked at Kay Glynn and she, in turn, smiled at me. And I said, *Wow.* Said it in my head, mind you. I don't think it would have been all that smart to blurt out, "Wow!" when some girl is looking at you.

And she was indeed some girl. Kay was blond, very pretty. She was an only child. Her father, old Charlie Glynn, owned a bicycle shop that also carried the best hardware in the city— knives, tools and things like that. He was also a wizard of a locksmith. There wasn't anything about any safe that he didn't know about. Major cities such as Detroit would call him in if a bank vault went wrong. He was a brilliant guy, Charlie was . . . although he never liked Kay and me being together.

Unfortunately, old Charlie came to a terrible ending in his life, years later, after World War II. Some guy broke into his shop. Now, Charlie was a fighter, and he wasn't about to quietly let some thief come in and just help himself to whatever he wanted. But the intruder overwhelmed him, just beat him terribly. They caught the intruder, and he drew fifteen years in prison.

There are different kinds of prison, though, for Charlie became a prisoner of an injured brain, damaged during that horrible beating. He wound up being institutionalized.

And Kay was the only one who could get through to him. She would just hold his hand and say, "Dad . . . they want you to do something. Can you do it?" And he'd answer, or perhaps not. Sometimes he would mimic fighting the fight all over again.

But that was many years in the future, as I mentioned. All I knew was that Kay was wonderful, and she was my best girl. We became something of a regular item. Our favorite date would be to hitch a ride with older kids on a Friday or Saturday night and head over to Dell's Barbecue. We'd put nickels and dimes into the music box, the Wurlitzer, and just dance. Swing dancing at the time, and we were pretty good at it.

It was around that time that I also found myself, much to my surprise, taking to the stage.

Ever since I'd been young, I'd excelled at two things when it came to entertaining folks: the first was dialects, and the second was singing.

In terms of dialects and accents, I guess I was just born with a good ear. Even as a child, just to practice, I would read out loud, walking from the living room to the hallway, to the kitchen and the dining room, and back into the living room. And every time I went through a doorway, I'd change my accent or the tone of my voice.

I remember my father saying to my mother, "How does he know a Cockney accent?" I'd picked it up from a movie. Didn't know the name of it, just knew that I could imitate it.

Eventually I built my repertoire up to about twenty accents. These included six or seven British accents, Irish, Scots, and all sorts of variations—a Glasgow accent, for example, as compared to the Aberdeen I eventually used as Scotty.

In the United States and Canada, we generally speak in about five notes. The Irish and Scottish will speak in perhaps seventeen to eighteen notes, up and down and up. The Dutch are a bit more subdued and use about seven or eight notes.

As for my singing, I was a very good boy soprano. When I was thirteen, my mother wanted me to enter a contest that the Kiwanis would have, and I would always say, "Oh, c'mon, Mom, I don't want to do that stuff." Besides which, a guy named Jack Shirley pretty much won year after year anyway.

But I gave in to her, because I so adored her and because (not that I'd admit it) I loved to sing. She taught me all sorts of Irish songs. In order to prepare for the contest, I went to an organist at the Presbyterian church, who was a voice teacher. The song I had to prepare was Schubert's "Hark, Hark, the Lark," which was tricky because it started quite high.

Unfortunately, my voice picked right around that time to change. I wound up coming in second because I could no longer hit the high note. I went *"Urkkhh,"* and nothing came out. Some nuns tried to be consoling afterward, saying, "Oh, you were just nervous."

And I said, "No, I wasn't nervous—my voice is changing."

Most of my high school education was at a very big school called the Sarnia Collegiate Institute and Technical School. It was there that both my singing and knack for imitation came into play. Not that I had any long-term goal involving acting. I didn't have any long-term goals involving *anything,* really. But when people asked me to do something—such as get up on stage and help out with a show or somesuch—I was happy to go along with it.

When I was sixteen, I played the title role in *Robin Hood* in a school production. I had to sit around the campfire and sing:

> *Early one morning, just as the sun was rising*
> *I heard a blackbird in a tree pipe a song.*
> *Farewell, we're going, cold winds are blowing,*
> *but we'll back when the days grow long.*

I was also master of ceremonies two years in a row for the annual school show, where we'd put on skits that included me doing imitations of singers like Bing Crosby, Vaughn Monroe, and Russ Columbo. One year at the school show I started by doing an imitation of famous broadcaster Walter Winchell, using his standard opening of, "Good evening, Mr. and Mrs. North America and all the ships at sea . . ."

All of this willingness to go along with whatever was asked of me served to make me fairly popular at school. Plus I was certainly popular with Kay as well. We went together so regularly that everyone thought that Kay and I were married when we were seventeen or eighteen. Except we weren't, of course.

However . . .

For all the fun I was having on the stage, for all my popularity at school, the situation with my father's drinking had really gotten to me. Every day of my life, day in and day out, was like walking barefoot through a bed of tacks. I had to tread carefully, in order to make sure I didn't catch his attention in a negative manner. Most people consider home a refuge; there's something unspeakably lonely about having no one to whom one could turn.

By the time I was seventeen, my grades started to drop off. I wasn't doing homework. It was a hell of a depressing time. My father's drinking had wound up interfering with his work, and they pensioned him five years early because he was just too unmanageable.

Even though I had my brothers and sister, I didn't really think anybody was going to help me then. I thought all my problems were with my father, and nobody seemed to be feeling the same things I felt. Otherwise, I thought, they'd mention it to me, but they didn't.

I felt as if I was alone. I would sit in the living room sometimes and everything in that room would seem to move away from me, leaving me in a tiny little spot, highlighting my sense of isolation.

All the love and affection my mother put out was not enough. I guess, more than anything, I just wanted to get away. Ironically, in his youth my father wanted nothing but to get away from conditions he considered oppressive. So here he was, decades later, with a son who had the exact same desire.

As it turned out, Adolf Hitler provided me the opportunity. World War II was coming. And I knew that I was going.

4

Giving Hitler the Finger

WATCH *STAR TREK* CAREFULLY AND YOU'LL NOTICE SOMETHING rather odd about Mr. Scott.

You almost never see his right hand.

Most of the time it's not particularly obvious. After all, with Scotty and the rest of the crew of the *Enterprise* facing down planet killers, mad gods, mechanical changelings, and every other manner of intergalactic menace that the universe (with the help of a few writers) could devise, who spends a lot of time staring at Scotty's right hand?

In fact, you probably never even noticed the number of times that Mr. Scott would be sitting in the command chair of the bridge with his right hand tucked securely out of sight. Captain Kirk, when at that post, would reach up and tap the communications switches on the right armrest when he wanted to communicate to Scotty that more warp power was required, else the *Enterprise* would be free-floating atoms before the next commercial break.

But if Scotty, having taken command, paged Captain Kirk on planet surface to let the captain know about the latest crisis that threatened the ship, Scotty would oftentimes reach across his body with his left hand. The right remained obscured.

The reason was simple: Mr. Scott was missing the middle finger of his right hand. Why? Because Jimmy Doohan was likewise bereft of the same finger.

I was a bit self-conscious about it at the time, and one can't exactly put on digits as easily as one puts on accents. I'm not sure why I was self-conscious. I suppose it's because people do not like to see things that are not perfect. I think that's true of most audiences. I remember a live TV show I did called *Space Command* in Toronto. I was having lunch with one of the cameramen—we had already done forty-eight out of the fifty-two shows we would wind up shooting—and he said, "My God, what happened to your finger?!"

I told him, in graphic detail, how I'd lost it during my service in the army. And he said, "You mean I've seen you with your hands so many times, I've photographed those hands, and I never noticed it?"

"I guess so. I probably hide it on you."

There are a couple of times when it's conspicuous—if you happen to be so bored with a *Star Trek* episode that you feel the need to pick up minuscule details (which, admittedly, *Star Trek* fans have been known to do from time to time). For example, in "The Trouble with Tribbles," Scotty walks into a room with a massive armload of tribbles. The right hand is exposed and the gap is evident. Then again, the questioning fan might assume that it was hidden from view because it was being munched on by a particularly aggressive tribble.

I should have a story for how Scotty lost his finger. Perhaps he made a mistake with a phaser and used the disintegrator . . . He fired and it was aimed at his finger. In which case he was lucky, since he could have lost the whole arm.

I became less concerned about it after a time. By the time we got to the famed *Star Trek* cement ceremony in front of Mann's Chinese Theater, I was so unconcerned about it that I did the imprint with my right hand when I could just as easily have reached over with the left.

People give me the Vulcan sign and I go, "That's a *V* and this is a *U*."

When, precisely, during my military service, did it happen? Did it catch in the treads of a tank while I was a tank commander? Get sliced off by a propeller during my time as an aviator?

No, no. Nothing that simple.

It happened during the invasion of Normandy on D day, possibly the most dramatic military maneuver of the twentith century.

Sit back, lasses and laddies, and I'll tell ye about it . . .

The family radio, which had been the sourse of so much entertainment and enjoyment throughout the years, slowly became something much more oppressive. It was our daily link to the activities of Adolf Hitler, Germany's warmongering führer. Year after year we wanted to believe that someone would stop the maniac, but every year brought some new abomination from Hitler or his allies. In 1935 the Italians attacked Ethiopia. The Germans remilitarized the Rhineland in 1936, and there was the notorious Anschluss, the "annexing" of Austria, of 1938. Plus word was reaching us of what was happening to the Jewish population.

Yet, there was Neville Chamberlain, prime minister of England, on September 30, 1938, making an address from 10 Downing Street after returning from the Munich peace conference. "For the second time in our history," he declared in a burst of self-congratulation, "a British prime minister has returned from Germany bringing peace with honor. I believe it is peace for our time."

And as I heard this over the radio, I said, "Bull. You don't have any idea what this guy, Hitler, is after. He's going to take over everything if you don't stop him now."

My mother was a very, very loving woman who didn't want

anything bad to happen to anyone, Jew or Christian. She was a true lover of humanity. It was the Catholic church that helped her be that. But even a true lover of humanity like my mother was disgusted by what she saw from Hitler.

Now, my father, he viewed Hitler with a sort of military mentality. If anything, he regretted that he wasn't able to go in and help defeat him. For once, my father and I were on the same wavelength. Make no mistake, we would have *liked* to think that peace in our time was imminent, but I don't think the great majority of people at that point believed it at all.

Unfortunately, not everyone in Canada had philosophies along the lines of that of my family's. Many did not believe that Canada should get involved in the European conflict, no matter what the reports or whispered rumors might be of Hitler's activities.

It's not easy to hang blame on them. You should understand the makeup of Canada at the time. Half of the country's population of eleven million lived on farms or in small towns, and they had been very, *very* hard hit by the Great Depression. Unemployment was at around twenty-five percent, and even though by the late 1930s there had been some recovery, it was only some. Things were still difficult, and now there we were, barely two decades past the end of what had been called the Great War (who thought to call it World War I at the time?), and there was all sorts of discussion about getting involved in another worldwide conflict. Add to the mix that about half the population was British in origin, and another three million or so considered themselves French, and you can understand the incredible interest and worry about the European conflict.

But eventually it came down to the final straw. Barely a year after the Munich agreement Chamberlain had crowed about—September 1, 1939, to be precise—Hitler invaded Poland. It became clear at that point, even to the most isolationist, that Hitler wasn't going to be deterred by agreements and signed pieces of paper. Modern-day science fiction movie fans would liken him to the Terminator: he couldn't be bargained with; he couldn't be reasoned with; he would just keep destroying and destroying until someone stopped him.

The two someones who resolved to do so were Britain and France, telling him to get out of Poland immediately. Hitler, in his arrogance, ignored them, and on September 3 they declared war. The Canadian Parliament began to debate a resolution for war while the First and Second Canadian Divisions began the first stages of mobilization.

On September 10, 1939, Canada officially joined the war effort.

I was the eleventh guy to join up in Military District #1. My army number was A17111.

The Canadian army, as it was set up during peacetime, consisted of two divisions, the militia and the Permanent Force. The militia existed primarily to keep volunteer soldiers meeting a couple of times a week to drill and learn things such as first aid. But there wasn't any truly serious training in the sorts of things required to stay alive on a field of battle.

The Permanent Force was the full-time, professional army, which was to train the militia and keep itself in a constant state of readiness. But even with both the militia and the PF combined, there couldn't have been more than one hundred thousand men nationwide who were involved in any serious sort of military training.

Now . . . it's not as if I enlisted simply because I saw it as a means of escaping my father. At age nineteen, other options could have presented themselves. Plus it would be bizarre to refer to the conquests of a megalomaniacal German dictator as serendipity. Getting away from my unhappy homelife was not my primary motivator, but merely a by-product. Nonetheless, it was a by-product that gave me a tremendous feeling of relief; a weight of years of oppression being lifted from me.

The bottom line was that I wanted to have a chance to do something about that Hitler guy. My mother just said, "Well, that's what you have to do." I knew she was frightened for me, but she just hugged me and that was all. She was never the most verbal of women.

My eldest brother, Tom, had moved to South America, but my brother Bill was a lieutenant in the militia. It had not been all that long before that I had been the best man at Bill's wedding. At that wedding, for a gift, he'd given me a silver cigarette case. It was absolutely a beautiful keepsake, and I brought it with me when I went to enlist. I hoped it would bring me luck.

It looked as if I was going to need it, because the fact of the matter was that the Canadian military was not in strong shape. As the Depression had worn on, the tiny core of military "might" that had been kept active had had its budget slashed to the bone. When a country is trying to keep its populace from rioting for food (which had occurred in some cities), keeping a healthy military during peacetime is simply not a high priority. Now it looked as if we were going to be paying for it, because everything from uniforms to rations was either in short supply or nonexistent. The only thing we had in any degree of supply was rifles.

Even our local enlistment office was a makeshift little place in an unused store. There was no boot camp, nowhere to train. Besides, how do you start training eleven men? My first contribution to the war effort was chauffeuring officers around.

I signed up for the duration of the war. There was no question of anything else. I mean, I didn't realize it would be six years and two months. Who knew? We could have declared war and then there could have been peace in two months.

In fact, that's what I expected. I had this notion that with England, France, and—of course—Canada joining the war, Hitler wouldn't be able to last very long. Oh, sure, I saw the Movietone News of Hitler's panzer division, and I knew we didn't have that kind of equipment. I often wondered if the people in the United States, right across the river, would ever get into this war. I ultimately concluded, no way. They might offer us some aid, but there was no way they were going to really get their hands dirty. But I figured we weren't going to need them, because faced with the mounting resistance of the European community, Hitler had to cave.

How could I have known? How could I know that I was signing away the next six years of my life? If I had it to do all over again, I'd do the same thing . . . but, good Lord, the enormity of it is so daunting that it was a fortunate thing I *wasn't* giving it any thought. I was a nineteen-year-old who had spent much of his life being intimidated and frustrated. And now I was being thrust into a situation unequipped, untrained, and—as it turned out—eventually given the responsibility for the lives of other men. *The lives of other men.* I no longer had the option of hiding in my cot or rocking in the corner of a room and isolating myself. I had to learn, as quickly as I could, how to handle myself in an assortment of life-and-death situations and eventually how to get men to follow my orders.

I gave no thought to the notion that I might get wounded or killed. That was secondary to the concern that I keep my head above water in the day-to-day challenge of dealing with other men in the army, both those above me and, eventually, those below me. Once I was trained, I wondered, would I be able to do everything the way I'd been trained? And, for that matter, if given the assignment of training others, could I do that job as well? Their lives might very well depend on the quality of my training.

And most important, of course . . .

How the hell do I break it to Kay?

Kay and I had become a pretty serious item. Serious enough, as I said earlier, that some people thought we were already married. But we never discussed getting married, possibly because her mother was trying to find ways to get us apart. Probably Charlie, Kay's dad, had asked her to do that. They didn't succeed in disrupting the love we felt for each other, but they did manage to send her off to Whitby College, on the other side of Toronto, two hundred miles from Sarnia. It was difficult for me to go there, for I had no job and no means of getting money to make the trip.

If times had been different, I might have been able to solve both problems. But as it was, while Kay had gone straight from high school into college, I had gone right from high school into the army. The war had presented itself, rudely back-burnering any plans we might have been clinging to.

I wrote her a letter, informing her I had joined the Royal Canadian Artillery. We wrote letters in those days if we wanted to communicate anything of any substance; telephones were just for quick delivery of information.

It may have been one of the single most important letters I ever wrote. Kay seemed to take it well, but I couldn't help but wonder how it felt to get such a major fait accompli delivered in the mail.

Five years later, I'd have the opportunity to find out. But that was five years into the future, and it would be a long, rocky road to get there.

5

You're in the Army Now

AFTER ABOUT SIX WEEKS, AROUND TWO HUNDRED MEN HAD enlisted. We were brought out to Bright's Grove on the shores of Lake Huron, which was no more than five miles from my home. Rather than barracks, they had us in summer cottages, sleeping twelve men to a cottage. I'll say one thing for a catch-as-catch-can army, some aspects can be fairly cushy. After all, why waste precious materials building barracks when the cottages were already there?

I had the rank of private, what we called a gunner. The immediate ranks of concern to me, from the bottom up were as follows: gunner, lance bombardier (a one striper), corporal bombardier (a two striper), and lance sergeant (three striper). Basically, they were all noncoms, noncommissioned officers. The lance sergeant is the most junior of all sergeants, with the highest rank being the regimental sergeant major—a very powerfully ranked individual and not one on whose bad side you'd want to get.

The militia organized men into regiments, basing the practice on the way the British army set up their territorial regiments. These "local" regiments, eventually consisting of two thousand men each, emphasized maintaining separate identities on a regional basis, encouraging a sense of family bonding and territorial pride. I was part of the Fourth Field Regiment, and part of our battery was made up of people from around the Guelph area and Kitchener (which was a big German area; in fact, before World War I, it was called Berlin). The regiments themselves were divided into batteries, each battery consisting of two troops of one hundred men each.

One thing I did was start to learn Morse code. After learning the basics, the practice was really quite straightforward. I would be sent, via Morse code, an entire newspaper—all the articles, every single day. And I would sit there and transcribe. It was the simplest, most straightforward way to build up my speed. I got up to forty-five words a minute eventually. My skill at Morse put me in a position to join the signal part of the artillery. It meant that we would be responsible for stringing telephone lines and such from the observation post to the guns, and then out to regiment headquarters.

My first problems in the regiment came as a result of the very brother who had been so good to me in the past. William had joined the militia some years earlier and, by the time of my enlistment, had risen to the rank of lieutenant. Because William was a lieutenant in the same outfit, there was a good deal of prejudice against me. In fact, sometimes it seemed that some guys were going out of their way to show they weren't intimidated by my "connections."

A routine cleanup job, for example, would result in the man who'd assigned it to me claiming it hadn't been done to his satisfaction. He'd bait me into a fight, and being a young hothead determined to show that I *didn't* need my older brother to cover my butt, I'd lay into him. Unfortunately, I wasn't smart enough to take on people smaller than myself. That time, and many other times, I always went toe-to-toe with someone bigger, and I always got the snot beaten out of me.

Yet, believe it or not, it eventually worked for me. I'd stand up for myself, and they'd kind of like me after that. After pounding the crap out of me, they could say, "Hey, he's a regular guy."

Kay would come and visit me whenever she was able to get a weekend off. And it did entail an entire weekend, because her college was so far away. Though I'd been in the army for only a few months, I was starting to change in small ways (if one doesn't count getting my face rearranged in fights.) Once I was at a dance with a friend of Kay's named Adelle Patton. And as we were dancing, I casually reacted to something in mild surprise by saying, "What the fuck—?"

Now, that's standard army talk, but I had never used it at home. I'd never spoken that way in my civilian life, particularly not at home and most particularly not in female company.

Adelle looked up at me in utter shock from the profanity that had dropped from me. I got so embarrassed that I tripped—whether it was over my own feet or Adelle's, I couldn't be sure. There was no doubt, however, as to what I instinctively grabbed for support to avoid falling—Adelle's rather copious breasts.

My skin went beet red, and I was so mortified that I just turned, walked away, and kept on going.

The most gorgeous thing I remember about that time was the trumpeters. In the Canadian artillery, you don't have buglers, you have trumpeters. Two trumpeters would play, one melody and one harmony. Whether it was blowing mess call or reveille, I swear to you it was the most gorgeous music I ever heard.

I got the first test of whether my bunk mates were going to cut some slack to the punching-bag brother of the lieutenant when I acquired a white, short-eared terrier. She was a gift, which was considerate, except that getting her was the army regs equivalent of being given a live grenade. Pets were not exactly standard issue. I kept her in my bed at night, and the other eight guys watched my efforts to shush the little fur ball with desperate pleas of, *"Shh!* Don't let anybody know you're here!"

The guys didn't rat me out, and I managed to keep her under wraps for five solid weeks . . . until Sergeant Major Richardson tumbled to her during an inspection and I was ordered to get rid of her. Fortunately, I found a nice family to take care of her.

It was just in time, as it turned out, because after six months of basic training, right around my twentieth birthday in 1940, I was informed I'd be shipping off to England to Camp Borden, where we would concentrate on nothing but signaling. Catchphrases such as "The walls have ears" and "Loose lips sink ships" may seem like just cute phrases nowadays, but back then they were words to live by. I couldn't even give specifics to my parents.

I was faced with a thousand-mile train trip to Halifax, during which time a fellow named Fox and I would fight the boredom by hanging out with the engineer and fireman. (Ironically, Fox had grown up five houses away from me, but I'd never played with him as a kid.) We'd ask if we could ride up front, and they'd say, "Sure!" because they'd do anything for the soldiers bound for overseas.

So there we were in our battle dress, which was khaki green, with a short jacket that had buttons up the front. And we rode in that cab for about 125 miles, speeding along at 70 miles per hour, the engine lurching tremendously and even frighteningly from side to side. The fireman kept shoveling coal, and I would pull the whistle to signal our coming. It was an incredible sensation: I'd gone from being a child, dreaming of escape while windup trains danced in front of my face, to a twenty-year-old with Canada racing past him, bound for an international journey to fight (dare I say it?) the forces of evil.

From Halifax it was a nine-day trip aboard a tramp steamer

to Liverpool, sailing on an Atlantic Ocean that was as smooth as a pond. It was the first time I had ever been on a ship, and I was . . .

Bored. Bored, bored, bored out of my mind. I'd walk around the deck, and that was the extent of my search for amusement, walking about dressed in my greatcoat, hat, and a khaki scarf. Never wore gloves. I would stand there, breathing in the salt air and watching my breath come out in mist, keeping an eyeball peeled for German subs and spotting nothing except, a couple of times, whales (which did set my heart to racing since German subs were painted to resemble whales).

Didn't even get down to the engine room, which is a terrible sin for Scotty to admit.

Indeed, a large measure of army life threatened to be tedious if I didn't do everything I could to stave off that deadly dull routine. Just as I had wanted to escape the things in my life that held me back, I had found something new to try and break away from, boredom.

But still . . . it felt as if we were going to war rather than just taking a dull ocean voyage. Two things really brought that home to me. First it wasn't as if we were alone. We were part of a convoy of eight ships, including such massive battleships as the H.M.S. *Repulse.*

And second, when we were a few of days away from our destination, a couple of dots appeared in the sky. It quickly became clear that they had targeted us. There were, standing on the rocking deck as the planes came closer and closer. There was a long, uncertain moment that seemed to stretch out forever.

It would have been a hell of a way for my war effort against Hitler to end . . . before it started, in essence. The notion of my possibly getting killed had never been a major factor to me, but it seemed such an utter waste—to have finally gotten out of my oppressive home situation, to be finally doing something with my basically aimless life, and to wind up as so much scrap on the Atlantic Ocean. . . .

Then the planes came fully into view. Rather than seeing the Luftwaffe, we found ourselves staring up at huge four-engine Sunderland flying boats. They were on our side, coming to check us out.

With the immediate "threat" aside, I had another chance to envy and admire the freedom of air flight. It seemed glorious and exhilarating and the stuff of fantasy for a young man from Sarnia whose life had been occupied by very earthbound, mundane concerns.

Once in England, we boarded an English train (much smaller than our sturdier Canadian steam engines designed for pulling through mountains). I was posted to Camp Borden, which was about sixty miles southwest of London. And there . . .

I waited. And waited some more. The army was the greatest waiting station in the world. Camp Borden? Camp Boredom was more like it. We were stuck going to pubs, eating fish and chips, and drinking warm British bitter beer. We'd work out at rifle ranges with our Lee-Enfield rifles, capable of accuracy at up to fifteen hundred yards, and I was pretty good with it. But riflery and marching was the extent of my "combat training," constituting maybe an hour each day. I was in the Signal Corps, after all. No one was expecting me to storm a German encampment and take down a half dozen Kraut guards with my bare hands.

Which wasn't a half bad fantasy, when you got into it. Me, I was glad that I had signed up for the Signal Corps. I loved the idea of laying wire, of communicating, of sending Morse code, of being in contact with others.

Perhaps it was a logical extension of my youth. So many years I had spent with violence hanging over me. So many years, there had been a sense of isolation. Upon joining the army, it seems natural in retrospect that I would tend to steer clear of positions designed for directly inflicting violence. Defend myself, yes, of course. I'd have had to be pretty stupid to go into a combat situation not having learned that. But, my father's violent nature must have drilled into me a healthy distaste for that state of mind.

So there had been young Jimmy Doohan—feeling alone, wishing he could find someone with whom he could converse—becoming young James Doohan, part of the Signal Corps of the army, entrusted with responsibility for maintaining open lines of communication.

But while I was busy polishing my Morse code transmission skills (still doing the transcription of the daily news) and taking target practice, things were not looking too good for the Allies. In mid-1940, we learned that our forces were being driven back in France. Thanks to panzer divisions coming in fast and furious, the Allied troops were being forced down practically to the beach at Dunkirk. By the beginning of June, the beach was overrun by the Germans. Although I wasn't at that battle, I not only heard about it but saw those exhausted, dirty, unshaven soldiers on trains the next day. Dunkirk was a devastating defeat, and you could see it in the faces of the English people. They were thinking, "God, this is it . . . this is terrible."

It was my first face-to-face experience with the true horror of war. And it wouldn't be the last.

6

Waiting for Action

I MET THE VOCAL INSPIRATION FOR MONTGOMERY SCOTT WHEN, after five weeks in England, I'd been relocated to Catterick Camp in Yorkshire, some 230 miles north of London. There, in living quarters that consisted of a metal hut with a round roof, was a fellow from Aberdeen named Andrew.

I couldn't understand a damned word he said.

Some people make snide comments, saying that Scotty's accent is inaccurate, that it's not authentic. Believe me, if I did it the way Andrew from Aberdeen did, you too would not understand a damned word Scotty said. In fact, Gene Roddenberry pulled me aside early in the series—several times, in fact—and said, "You mustn't make the accent so thick. No one's going to know what you're saying." Typical writer—wanting to make sure everyone understands those words, words, words!

All of which is a roundabout way of saying that it took me about a week of asking, "What does that mean?" to pierce his accent. It was painful for him too; trying to get through to me was like trying to explain particle physics to a newborn. Curiously, though, he understood everything I said.

We in the Signal Corps continued to train in all forms of communication and laying down wire. I was also pressed into service as a driver, since I had a license, something that not many young British people had. So there I was, my first time behind the wheel in an English army vehicle, with about seven or eight guys in the back . . .

You can probably see it coming. Yes, that's correct—I forgot that in England, you drive on the left side of the road. As per habit, I shot down the right side of the road; then, as I rounded a long curve, I saw a big, red double-decker bus bearing down on us at about fifty miles an hour.

Here I was trying to inspire confidence in my peers, and instead I managed to arouse stark terror as they screamed, *"What are you doing? What are you doing?!"* I swerved like crazy, locking eyes with the oncoming bus driver, and then I was just barely, just *barely,* out of the way.

That was my last bit of major excitement for the next nine months. I hit my twenty-first birthday, having spent a year and a half in the army, killing time as I waited for more members of my regiment to finish training and make the pilgrimage to England.

More and more Canadians were massing in England, with close to 78,000 Canadian men joining the active force. The main thing we were being prepped for was a possible full-scale invasion of London by the Germans.

This didn't seem an impossibility, for we were in the midst of the Battle of Britain—a brutal series of air raids against London that started in the summer of 1940, intensified around September of that year, and carried through to the spring of 1941. Essentially, the Luftwaffe was struggling with the RAF (Royal Air Force) for control of the skies over Britain.

Despite the danger, I visited London every weekend, if for no other reason than to spend time with my grandmother (having finally been given permission to inform my family of my whereabouts).

During one of my visits to London, I met a wing commander who was stationed at Bigham Hill, which was a big fighter airdrome. "Why don't we see if we can get you in sometime?" he asked. "Next week I expect to be quite busy, but I'm sure I can get you in."

So I went to Bigham Hill, and it was incredible. I'd watch those Spitfires take off, soaring toward altitudes of 23,000 feet to do battle with the Germans' twin-engine bombers, moving at speeds in excess of three hundred miles an hour. Spitfires would leap into the sky for three, four, five trips a day. There were two pilots in particular who caught my attention. They couldn't have been more dissimilar in style as each would come down from his plane and wait for the mechanics to get their respective fighters refueled and rearmed. One pilot, whom we'll call Alpha, would chat with the mechanics and then go off to lie down on the grass and nap. The other pilot, "Bravo," was on top of the mechanics. He'd be fussing around, checking this, probing that, urging them to hurry it up because there were battles to be fought and Germans to stop.

And I watched it all with a sort of incredulity. Alpha and Bravo were hardly demigods; they were men, just like me, with their own quirks and personality ticks. And for the first time, I watched with a new sort of slant to my thinking. One that dared to toy with the notion that maybe somehow, *some*how, that could be me—that I could climb into a cockpit and leap into the air. Going toe-to-toe with Luftwaffe pilots wasn't within the range of my ambition, but the chance to leave the difficult earth far behind . . .

For the first time, it started to seem like just that, a chance.

Month after month passed, and we trained and trained, and trained some more, moving to a place outside the town of Horsham in the southern part of England, and from there to a town called Hastings, where the Battle of Hastings was fought in 1066. And as 1941 rolled on into 1942, as the war continued, we Canadians were going out of our minds. *Why aren't they using us?* we were wondering.

We weren't the only ones. While British and French forces fought and died against the Germans, while France had fallen before Hitler's troops, people back home in Canada were hungry to read of the efforts of the Canadian forces against Hitler. But there was nothing to read, and the populace of Canada started to grow angry. Our forces had been deployed; why wasn't anything being *done* with them? We in England were asking the same questions.

The answer lay with Major General A.G.L. McNaughton, one of the top men in the Canadian military. McNaughton strongly believed that the Canadian troops should be deployed as a unit. Anywhere we were to go, we were to go en masse.

This presented two difficulties. Remember, part of our training had been to provide defense for England itself. To take us all away in one shot would be a major blow to the security of England. Plus the logistics of transporting all of us in one shot made it an impossible undertaking.

And so we drilled ourselves silly.

I was now twenty-two years old, and even though the passage of time had brought me up to the rank of lance sergeant—the cheapest form of sergeant, ranking just above a corporal—I was still chomping at the bit.

I killed time with my best friend, a Norton motorcycle on which I logged more than sixty thousand miles. I only had a couple of mishaps, including one when I was part of a convoy on the way to Wales. I came around a curve at seventy miles an hour and suddenly saw in front of me—no, not a double-decker bus—but rather, a pothole about five feet long and six inches deep. With no way of avoiding it, I jumped the hole. I prayed while I was airborne, the momentum carrying me, and I managed to keep my front wheel straight, which was the only thing that saved me. I landed on my rear wheel, which bounced back and forth and then straightened out.

We'd also practice infantry fire, using twenty-five-pounder guns—so called for their twenty-five-pound shells—very efficient, highly praised weapons. Practice involved a system peculiar only to the British army called quick concs, which was short for "quick concentrations" of infantry barrages that made the entire ground just erupt. The system was created by the same Major General "Andy" McNaughton who was keeping us sitting around on our asses while Hitler rampaged around the European theater.

There were these and other diversions, but I wasn't interested in diversions anymore. It had gone beyond just wanting to take on Hitler. My unfortunate home situation now was both physically and emotionally distant. You can only run away from something for so long before you have to start running *toward* something.

Which is why I was thrilled to learn that my colonel was willing to recommend me to Officers Training School.

My initial interview was held at Billingshurst with General Odam from Vancouver. He asked me general textbook questions, which required only a regurgitation of the facts that I'd had drilled into me during the two and a half years I'd been in the service. But it seemed as if my answers were only secondary to my overall look, which was deemed by General Odam as "too young." I had something of a baby face, and Odam must have felt that the men under me wouldn't take me seriously.

But about four weeks later, they began a new system where they subjected officer candidates to a special general-knowledge exam, a psychological exam, etc. I arrived at a gymnasium to discover about five hundred guys, all taking the exam, out of which only about sixty would be chosen. I spent the next three hours carefully filling out the predominantly multiple-choice exam.

About three weeks later I was called in front of General Odam. I stood there in his office, looking at him with an even gaze as he scrutinized me and said, "I remember you. I turned you down before."

I said, "Yes, sir."

He told me reluctantly, "Well, you got top score in the tests, so I'm forced to allow you to become an officer."

Keep in mind, this didn't mean that General Odam had necessarily been wrong in his assessment. I did look exceedingly young, my features hardly the sort of chiseled-from-stone image that commands instant obedience. My work was going to be cut out for me, getting troops of strong-willed Canadians to snap to when the baby-faced boy from Sarnia told them what to do.

Before officers school, which was to be held in the south of Manchester, they drilled us through six weeks of infantry training. That's where I truly learned how to fight. They taught me what infantry was all about and how exciting it could be.

We watched demonstrations of seasoned troops. For example, as we stood up on a mound, our attention would be drawn to forty soldiers standing about half a mile away. The only thing between them and us was a lot of four-foot-high scrub grass and maybe some swamp water.

At a signal, these forty guys descended into the scrub. We watched the scrub, looking for some sort of rustling, our eyes straining to pick up the slightest movement. There was nothing, and we started to wonder what the purpose of the exercise was. To watch forty soldiers hide in the brush without moving? Nice ambush tactic, but nothing much beyond that.

Twenty minutes later a whistle was blown, and I swear to you, when they rose up out of the brush . . .

Let me put it to you this way: Take this book, hold it at arm's length and then pretend it's an infantryman's rifle barrel pointed right in your face. We had not seen so much as the slightest movement.

And don't even get me started on the Canadian-Scottish regiment that the Germans called the "Ladies from Hell." Yelling, screaming, and shouting, they charged toward us for demonstration purposes with their rifles extended and their bayonets gleaming in the light. Then they stopped three feet in front of us and lowered their rifles. They couldn't have cut it any thinner. Another step or two and we would've been speared. Thank God they were on our side.

Our schooling was held in a castle called Alton Towers, a big castle on the moor. There was a stairway behind the castle that led to the nearest pub. Unfortunately, the stairway was 280 steps long! The bad news was that it took forever to get to the pub. The good news was that if you were returning with a snootful, by the time you'd climbed all the way back up, you were stone-cold sober again.

I made friends with one Hal Cross from Newfoundland, and together we found a nice old lady who was willing to rent us out study space. She'd bring us tea at nine o'clock at night, with stuff she had baked, boysenberry pie, cakes, things like that.

During the six months of training, we learned about everything from maneuvering a tank to firing artillery. I kept my mimicking of accents sharp by imitating what I heard around me. Most memorably, I once aped our main instructor's thick accent by repeating an order back to him during one artillery practice. He ordered me to launch "Three rounds, gunfire, fire!" And I repeated the order back to him using his exact pronunciation: "three rounds, gunfah, fah!"

"Oh, I say, Doohan, good ol' chap!" He grinned, breaking out into laughter. He might not have taken it in such good stride if he hadn't just gotten himself engaged to one of the richest young women in England. I figured it was best not to push his good humor, though, and so never did it again.

We had all sorts of things to learn. We had to know about medium guns, about heavies, and what they did. We were shown examples of these things and their ranges. Six months later, in August of 1942, I graduated at the age of twenty-two. Shortly thereafter I received my commission of lieutenant from the governor-general of Canada.

My first job was aide-de-camp—a kind of confidential assistant and secretary—to the Second Corps general. He was involved in inspecting the Second Division (consisting of 12,000–15,000 men), which was preparing for a strike on a highly fortified French seaport town called Dieppe. There was tremendous pressure for some sort of action to be taken on the western front; despite the philosophy of wanting to keep all the Canadian troops together, the folks at home were becoming as frustrated with the inactivity as the troops themselves were.

This home-front pressure dovetailed with British concerns, since the British wanted to know whether there was a radar station on Dieppe. They wanted to determine whether German radar technology matched their own.

To cut a long story short, the attack on Dieppe was not only a disaster, it was the single greatest loss of Canadian forces in the war. The commandos did accomplish one aspect of their mission, ascertaining that the Germans didn't have much of anything in the way of radar in Dieppe. But, good God, at what a cost was that discovery made. I wasn't involved in the actual fighting in that raid, and it was a good thing. If I had been, the odds would have been against my making it back, because of the nearly five thousand men who took part in the actual attack, less than half that number returned.

Yet, the knowledge that my comrades were putting their lives on the line while I had not seen any action was preying on me. Plus the Dieppe fiasco wasn't exactly conducive to the assignment of more Canadian troops to maneuvers, which meant a future of more boring, routine details for me to attend to.

Finally, I went to the general and said, "Please, there's not enough for me to do here; would you send me to a regiment?"

He did. He shipped me off to the Thirteenth Field Regiment in Horsham in the southwest of England (more east than Camp Borden), which had been drawn from the militia around Regina, Calgary, and Edmonton in Canada.

And thirteen was certainly unlucky for me.

Despite the fact that I had been in the army now for *three years,* I was still raw when it came to commanding men. After all, soldiers respect men who know the ropes—men who have the experience, the grizzle, the years, and the mileage. And here I was, fresh out of Officers Training School, having not dodged so much as a bullet, not stared down a single German gun, not spent a single moment with my neck on the line.

To make matters worse, there was already a sort of chain-of-nepotism in existence at the Thirteenth that threatened to break the chain of command (of which I was not, admittedly, the strongest link). There was a gunner under my command whose father ran a hardware store back home, and the major who was over me worked for the gunner's father back in civilian life!

Consequently, if I gave the gunner an order that he didn't like, he'd go behind my back to the sergeant major. The sergeant major would take it to the major, and the next thing I knew, the major would step in and rescind the order.

This quickly became a bad situation. And it escalated as the gunner started getting my orders rescinded not just for himself, but as a sort of "courtesy" to the others. I did a routine kitchen inspection and couldn't even get the kitchen cleaned up to snuff.

Exasperated, I went to Colonel Sparling, head of the Thirteenth, and told him the situation. "Sir, we are going to have a lousy regiment."

"Don't worry, Doohan," he told me with assurance. "We'll do something about that."

I wasn't quite sure what he would do, but I was sure he was going to call the major on the carpet or perhaps ream out the sergeant major. Maybe he'd line up the whole damned troop and tell them that they'd better snap to when Lieutenant Doohan barked an order, by God.

Instead he transferred *me*.

I suppose, to him, it made sense. Everyone else was functioning just fine; it was this wet-behind-the-ears lieutenant who seemed to be having problems. So he punted me over to another battery under another major, putting me in as the gun position officer (GPO).

And the same darn thing started to happen.

This time it wasn't a case of someone working for someone's father. No, in this case I was being treated as damaged goods. A tank driver named Corrigan chatted it up with my previous battery, and word was already out: Lieutenant Doohan could be gotten around. The seniors thought nothing of rescinding his orders. I was supposed to be a troop leader in charge of between sixty to seventy men, and I was getting no respect from them. Perhaps it arose from the fact that I had been primarily trained in communications work but—because I had risen in rank—was overseeing men whose expertise was artillery.

They must have figured that I didn't have the resolve, the pluck, or the experience to try to overcome any resistance on their part. In other words, they figured they could push me around. Indeed, they were in a perfect position to do so, because now my back was against the wall. Was I supposed to complain to Colonel Sparling *again*? Crab about yet another sergeant major going over my head, yet another battery that felt my orders could be questioned? I sensed that Colonel Sparling was already uncertain about my ability to command my men. The last thing I needed to do was give him more reason for doubt.

I railed in my own mind against the unfairness of it all. Then I realized I was back in the same old situation—lacking control. And it burned me, because when I was a kid, my father was my "superior officer." Here I had subordinates, and I couldn't even get *them* to snap to.

And as my anger grew, it prompted a brain wave.

Every morning each tank and gun driver had certain maintenance chores to accomplish before breakfast: warm up the engine, check the oil, the periscopes, etc. I went to the sergeant major one day, and, sounding as if nothing extraordinary was planned, I pulled out a map and said, "Tomorrow morning, Corrigan and I are going to go to the South Downs, through the town of Bournmouth, and climb to the South Downs by this road. We'll be gone most of the day. Special maneuvers."

That night, about one o'clock, I went down to my troop's vehicles, kept myself hidden from the guards, went up to my tank, and put black tape over the periscopes, and then went back to bed. By six the next morning, Corrigan had taken his place inside the tank, down in the turret.

I did everything I could to keep my voice steady, because I didn't want to tip Corrigan to the fact that something was up. "The engine's already warm, Corrigan. Let's move out as soon as possible. Let me know when you're ready."

He started it up. I kept my fingers crossed. If he noticed at this point, I'd be obligated to let him remove the visual obstruction, probably even have to commend him on following procedures correctly. I called, "Are you ready?"

"Yes, sir!"

Bingo. He'd reported to his superior officer that he was ready, willing, and able to take the tank out. I had him. "Okay, hard left!" I said, cool as you please.

Then he paused and said, very puzzled, "Excuse me, sir, I can't see."

Sternly I demanded, "What do you mean you can't see?"

"I just can't see."

Driving the point home, I said, "That means you didn't inspect your periscopes."

"Yes, sir, I guess so."

"Well, if you had, Corrigan, you'd have noticed that someone—to be specific, me—put tape over the periscopes. But you didn't, and now it's too late. You're going to follow my orders on when to change gears, when to turn left, right, hard left, hard right, whatever. I'll tell you when to stop, when to change gears, what to change up to, what to change down to. You're going to be driving blind, Corrigan."

I heard him mutter, "Oh, shit." I was never happier to hear those two words in my life.

Tanks ride fairly smoothly, but they're noisy as hell. I kept in communication with Corrigan through a microphone, sounding as calm as if I had icewater in my veins as I informed him, "We are going to go up the South Downs and through the traffic in Bournmouth. That's *lots* of traffic, Corrigan. So please do not make a mistake."

Well, he made four or five mistakes. Fortunately it was small stuff—not changing gears fast enough, stalling out. Nothing quite as catastrophic as rolling over a vehicle or person, which, in retrospect, was pretty damned lucky for all concerned.

We got to the South Downs by about eleven-thirty, where I promptly took a half-hour nap. And that was probably a fairly long half hour for him, because he could have removed the tape during that time. Except I hadn't ordered him to do so, and since the entire demonstration was an exercise in the importance of following orders, he knew he'd get me angry if he started acting contrary to my wishes. We were isolated, alone, and there was no sergeant major for Corrigan to go running to, no superior officer to rescind my order. It was just me, him, and a Sherman tank.

When I awoke from my nap, the tape was still on the periscope. Perhaps he was hoping that his having left it on would appeal to my good nature. But after weeks of having army boots marching all over my self-esteem, there wasn't much good nature to appeal to. "Now," I informed him, "I'm going to get down below and I'm going to drive the tank, and *you're* going to tell *me* what to do." I heard a moan from him. He didn't know that I had had a six-week course as a tank driver. Fortunately for him (and for myself, I suppose), I didn't make a mistake.

The moment we got back, word circulated through the battery of what had happened. It got around so fast you wouldn't believe it. The next morning I nailed the guards for being lax in their duty. After all, I had slipped past them and sabotaged a tank with impunity. They were confined to barracks for five days, unable to go into town, get a drink, or do anything except stare at each other and wish to God that no one had gotten Lieutenant Doohan quite this pissed off.

From then on, if I gave an order, it was obeyed just like that. I hadn't gone to the colonel, or the major, the captain, anybody. I straightened out the whole damn thing myself. I think that's probably one of the best things I've ever done in my life. I'm really proud of that.

I was also proud of my brother Bill. As 1942 rolled into 1943, and as we were kept on standby in England, my brother Bill was making a name for himself. He and others from the First Division, as well as other Canadian soldiers and officers, were attached to British forces in North Africa in order to garner battle experience. Their target was Erwin Rommel, the legendary German field marshal known as the Desert Fox. Bill had picked up his own nickname, the "Mad Major," since he was utterly daring and nothing seemed to faze him.

After dueling with Rommel's forces for three months, the Canadian First Division was the beneficiary of some of the home-front pressure for Canadian troops to become more involved in the war effort, rather than just sitting around training (as was our own company's status). The First Division was part of the summer 1943 attack on Sicily.

Bill was second-in-command of the regiment. One time he was out reconnoitering in a jeep, with a driver at the wheel. They were in pursuit of a squad of German soldiers who were in retreat. Bill got halfway across a bridge, and then the pursuit was abruptly terminated as the far end of the bridge was blown out. Quickly they tried to back up, but then the back end of the bridge was blown as well, and the whole thing—bridge, jeep, Bill, and his driver—went crashing down into the river. Undeterred, Bill and his driver managed to swim to shore. They didn't try to save the jeep, though—he was the "Mad Major," after all, not the Totally Insane Major.

By August of that year, Sicily had been taken, and the general consensus was that the First Division had acquitted itself well.

As for myself, I had been in the army for four years and had yet to be in the midst of a real combat situation.

That was about to change, for word was spreading of a major offensive being planned. The code name was Operation

Overlord, and the Germans knew it was coming. They just weren't sure where, although the smart money bet that it would be in Calais, at the narrowest part of the English Channel.

But, the invasion wasn't scheduled for Calais. That was a ruse foisted on them by the Allies. No, the attack was going to be further west—the beach at Normandy.

My first major battle experience was merely going to be as part of one the most significant military maneuvers of the twentieth century. By the time we finally reached D day—the invasion of Normandy—I would be celebrating (if one could call it that) my fifth year of service in the army.

I was twenty-four years old, and if the Germans had been marginally better shots, I wouldn't have made twenty-five.

7

D Day

WE TRAINED AND PREPARED FOR SIX WEEKS WITH THE ROYAL
Navy for Operation Overlord, a mission that it was hoped
would signal the beginning of a drive that would liberate
Europe. Overall the training had gone smoothly, except for
my encounters with one particular man, a coxswain—a
person who steers a boat. This coxswain was steering the
landing craft as we did practice runs, nearly half a dozen, to
gain experience with what was involved in making a land
assault. Some were against cliffs, others against low-lying
areas, but the consistent thing was that the coxswain continu-
ally disregarded my orders. I would tell him to steer in such
and such a direction or follow a particular course, and the
coxswain would just do whatever the hell he felt like.

This was singularly frustrating for me. I had thought I'd left
far behind me those days of insubordination from the lower
ranks. With this one coxswain, I was right back where I had
been a year and a half ago. I didn't quite know how to handle
it, and that was even more frustrating.

After that I rejoined my troop, and we were relocated to a

spot closer to Southampton, about one hundred miles from Bournmouth.

Two days before the D day invasion, Field Marshal Bernard Montgomery inspected our troops. It wasn't the first time. He'd been through back in 1942, checking out every Canadian division. But it was different this time, because we knew our entry into the war was imminent. We stood out on a large, abandoned airfield, and I brought the troops to attention with a bellowed order. Ten thousand Canadian troops snapped to at my command. Montgomery, as he walked down the aisle, nodded approvingly to me and said, "Good voice." That was a great moment for me.

Then he told us, "The Germans will counterattack on the morning of the third day, but in the meantime, you get in there and consolidate your position." Although I knew that we were going into war, it might have been at that moment that it all became truly "real" for me.

About three days before the intended strike at Normandy, a twin-engine German Dornier bomber flew overhead at eleven o'clock at night. To this day I'm certain that the bombardier didn't know we were encamped below. We were at full darkness; there was no way that he could have spotted us. He was flying at about four hundred feet. I suspect he just wanted to head home already, and he decided to dump his last bomb before heading back to Germany.

It was an incendiary bomb, and if the German bombardier had planned it, he couldn't have targeted us better. The damned thing landed smack in our ammo dump, and everything started going off.

The hero of the day was one Sergeant Brikofsky, who never lost his head, even as the intense heat from the incendiary bomb sent shells flying and popping all over the place. Instead, Brikofsky was leaping into tanks and moving them away from where everything was going off so that none of the tanks would be damaged.

In the end, we'd lost four guns and a full load of ammunition. Fortunately—even miraculously—we hadn't lost any lives. We'd been lucky; the bombardier could have dropped his bomb on some of our soldiers just as easily as on our ammunition. The army was so well-organized that less than twelve hours later, the division had replaced everything that had been lost. It was just ammo, after all—not human lives.

One would have been hard put to find anything positive in the slaughter that had taken place at Dieppe. But at least the high command had learned the hazards, indeed, the near impossibility, of trying to take a port city. Any sort of invasion was better advised to be on open beach.

The unfortunate Dieppe outcome had not deterred the Allies from their determination that France had to be liberated. Through 1943 and into 1944 the plans were made, the men and machines moved into position, and General Dwight David Eisenhower oversaw the entire operation. D day was selected as June 5, 1944, and if anyone in France had been operating on the assumption that there was no invasion planned, events during the two months prior to June 5 disabused them of the notion. British-based aircraft (including planes flown by Canadian forces) bombed the hell out of rail lines, bridges, and airfields. In order to cover the Normandy strike, a good deal of bombing was concentrated in the area of Calais, in northwest France, as well as the Normandy area, but on the Strait of Dover rather than the English Channel. This further confused the Germans.

We were fully brought up to speed a few days before the invasion, having been shown pictures of the shore taken by British motor torpedo boats with infrared cameras. I thought Normandy Beach was strategically a perfect spot—coming from near Portsmouth, as we were, Normandy was straight across. We weren't going to have to come in at an angle. It was the same direction for everybody.

The Allied forces' assault—176,000 men in all—was going to be made at five points along the beach code-named Utah,

Omaha, Gold, Sword, and Juno. I had been pulled from my own troops and given a command that consisted of 120 men in D Company of the Winnipeg Rifles. We were coming in at Juno, which was where the majority of Canadian forces were being committed.

We were brought aboard our ships as we watched the tanks also being loaded on: four gun tanks in front in two-by-two formation, followed by a Sherman tank. Some of the soldiers seemed a bit intimidated by the scope of the plan. Let's face it, the Dieppe massacre couldn't have been far from anyone's mind. But as we set sail for Normandy, the vast majority of the troops were utterly and commendably sanguine. Our attitude was, "This is it; this is what we've been training for; we're just going to follow orders and do it."

Still, during the day and a half that it took to get to our destination, it might have been possible for an air of grim determination—even fatalism—to have hung over the ship. It wasn't as if anyone was anxious to die or wanted to dwell on it. That way lay excessive morbidity, the kind of thinking that could undercut a troop's confidence. I'd been promoted to command post officer, (CPO) and the last thing I wanted was the morale of my troops undermined.

The seas of the Channel, moreover, were not the smoothest. In fact, the waters had been so choppy that D day had been moved back one day, to June 6.

So we *could* have dwelt excessively on the imminent battle and the German bombardment that might greet us when we set foot off the boat. Or we could—to put it appropriately—soldier on.

My men and I chose the latter, and consequently we spent almost every waking hour of our time on that boat playing craps. I swear to you, I cleaned out every crap game aboard that ship. I made 3,600 English pounds and kept it in my uniform at all times.

There was a certain irony in this, I suppose. I had no idea whether I was going to be alive to spend it within a couple of days. But at least I had a pocketful of money at that moment. No matter what happened on the beach, nothing could take that from me.

We floated on the English Channel for hours, seventeen miles off the Cherbourg peninsula, the beach at Normandy in sight. Matters aboard the boat had become very quiet. Each man was pensive, thoughtful, contemplating what was in front of him; each man trying to focus on the job for which he had been trained.

I thought also of home during that time, thought of my family. I thought of Kay Glynn. I didn't dwell on the possibility that I might not make it off the beach, because that way lay insecurity and even fear. That wasn't an option for me. Instead, as I lay there through the night, hour piling on upon hour, I thought about trying to live up to the example my brother Bill had set. I wanted to make my family proud of me.

And besides, even the passing of all the years hadn't diminished my youthful determination to make my own personal strike against Hitler and his plans. My patriotic fervor and pride in my country's efforts still burned brightly, and there was the blood of thousands of Canadians spilled at Dieppe to motivate us. My countrymen had fought and died in the struggle with Germany. If nothing else, I would do the best job I could in their memory.

We floated there, waiting for Eisenhower to give the final order to go. The sea bucked under us, a bit calmer than it had been, but still not mild enough to provide as easy a landing as we would have liked. We didn't know that Eisenhower, at the time, was considering pushing D day back three more weeks and was waiting until the last possible moment before making his decision.

Each minute stretched out to an ungodly amount of time, the shore was tantalizingly near. Sooner or later you reach a point where you just want to stop *thinking* about it, *anticipating* it, you just want to get out there and do the damned job.

Then word reached us, spreading throughout the ship with incredible speed. I think it was about four-thirty in the morning. And the word was, *It's go . . . We're a go,* and there was a rush of blood through me, adrenaline pumping, my jaw set and determined. For a giddy moment I wondered what my father would think of me if he could see me at that very instant; tried to picture the man who had haunted me and how he'd react to a battle-ready officer about to leap into combat with a hated enemy whom my father could only rail against from thousands of miles away. We were here to try to liberate France, and yet in a way, I had found my own means of personal liberation.

We clambered down rope ladders, down into the LCAs (landing assault crafts). I was in LCA #5 with thirty-three men of the total 120 under me, and I'd be damned if I'd lose any of them falling overboard while climbing into the LCAs. I kept careful watch to make sure all got aboard safely, although I did have help. There were men strapped to the ladders to assist us in climbing into the LCAs. The object was to get into the LCA without falling into the drink.

My troops were composed of my assistant, Chevalier, a tall, lanky, slow-moving guy; beach commandos; beach signalers; British engineers; and a Japanese sergeant from Singapore whose job was to blow up antitank mines. All were specialists, all experts in their fields.

In every direction, as far as you could see, right to the horizon, there was nothing but ships, ships, ships. Big, small, tiny, all sizes in between. It was a breathtaking sight. I had known intellectually what was going to be involved and the number of forces set to participate. I didn't see any American troops nearby, for they were at the westernmost entry points, at Utah Beach and Omaha Beach. Canadian and British troops were focusing on the easterly Gold, Juno, and Sword beaches. The First British Corps was overseeing the strikes on all three beaches. Juno itself was broken up into two subcategories, "Mike" and "Nan" beaches, with the Seventh Brigade and the Sixth Canadian Armored Regiment hitting Mike while the Eighth Brigade, along with the Tenth Canadian Armored Regiment struck at Nan. As noted, 176,000 men were divided up among the beaches.

But to know all this, to know the manpower involved, is one thing. To see this armed might floating all around us was something else altogether. War is never a joyous thing, but nonetheless there was a sort of beauty to it.

What wasn't beautiful was the identity of the man steering the LCA. It was the same coxswain who had given me all manner of grief during our practices. He looked at me in a way that basically said, *"Don't even try to give me orders; just shut up and stay out of my way."*

It was an intolerable situation; more than that, it was dangerous. In a combat situation such as what we were faced with, everyone had to be on the same page, and it has to be the command officer turning that page. I had to deal with the coxswain in an immediate and definitive manner, and only one way seemed open to me.

My brother Bill had given me two gifts that I always carried with me. One I mentioned earlier, the silver cigarette case. That was securely stashed in my vest pocket. The other was a pearl-handled .38 Smith and Wesson.

Without hesitation I pulled it and aimed it squarely at the coxswain's face. He blanched, and his eyes seemed to come together at the bridge of his nose. Sounding as calm as a headwaiter announcing a table, I said, "Look . . . you did not obey any order I ever gave you in all the practices we had. You better believe you are going to do it now, or I will take over the wheel."

His Adam's apple bobbed up and down slightly. There seemed to be the slightest thought in his mind that I was bluffing. I wasn't. As if reading his mind, I said, "I mean this. I am in charge of this boat, not you. You will do exactly what I tell you to do, and as soon as I tell you to do it."

He gave the barest of nods. Perhaps he was worried about making any sudden move, for fear that I'd just pull the trigger. "I will obey," he said tonelessly.

I put the automatic away, a bit relieved that things hadn't been pushed to a point of no return. It was terribly dangerous down there, because the Germans had built charming little barriers called hedgerows. They zigzagged somewhat in the water, and we had to maneuver carefully past them, because they had mines attached to them. The mines could easily blow us out of the water.

Daylight was starting to approach as the waves chopped us up and down. Fog was thick in the air, which I knew was a bad sign. With the area shrouded in fog, it handicapped the air force that was supposed to be providing us cover. The planes were supposed to swoop in and bomb the crap out of the beach to pave the way for us, to drive the Germans back. But impenetrable fog made such a plan problematic. If the planes stayed above the fog cover, their accuracy would be tremendously impeded. They could just as easily turn us into Canadian smoked meat as nail the Germans. But if they came in too low, they'd be making themselves extremely vulnerable to German antiaircraft fire.

The silence was eerie, the kind that penetrates your bones. Although we were a fighting team of army men, when it came to this kind of situation, every one of us was alone with his personal demons. I wondered what it was like for the other men. I wondered what there was in their backgrounds that had brought them to this moment. Was it the patriotism, or was it—in a time of depression—the steady job? I wondered if any of them really wished, at that very moment, to be anywhere but where they were.

I kept focusing on the job ahead. Once my troop was landed, the first thing we were supposed to do was survey the gun positions. We had to find the nearest and best-looking field in which to set up the guns. Guns that would be turned to fire upon the Germans and drive them further inland, away from Juno Beach. I was to coordinate with regimental survey officer and CPO Bob Waldie, as well as fellow CPO, Brownridge. Once we marked the positions for the guns . . . then we waited.

The nearest LCAs to our troops were the Regina Rifles. In the fog, I could barely see them.

My men did everything they could to deal with the constant rolling of the waves. It was like invading while inside a washing machine.

The silence was jolted by the sound of a British motor torpedo boat slashing across in front of us. He was just half out of the water, half submerged because of the waves. He was saying, "H hour minus thirty, H hour minus thirty." In other words, we were to wait another thirty minutes before we landed. I had no idea why the further delay; perhaps it was in the vain hope that the fog would lift. In any event, we cut across the waves that were coming in, then went back out into the waves, then across them again. Anyone who's ever been in a commercial aircraft that's circling an airport in a holding pattern, while being buffeted by turbulence, will have an idea of what the ordeal was like.

Finally, thirty minutes was gone. It was 7:15 A.M., and I said, "Let's head in. Full speed ahead."

The waves were still choppy as we maneuvered down the channel between the hedgerows, the waves apparently determined to try and shove us against the mines. We were all aware of the delicacy of the situation. The slightest bump up against one of the mines and we were going to hit the beach, all right . . . one piece at a time.

I had my men lie down in a mass, as close to the center of gravity as they could get. This, I believe, was a significant contribution to our survival. The Regina Rifles to our left lost three LCAs with all hands aboard, because—I believe—they didn't do what we did.

We just barely made it past the hedgerows and bumped up against the beach. All around us, Juno Beach was alive with a cacophony of violence. All along Normandy, the battleships had opened fire on the Germans to pave the way for our arrival. Shells blasted overhead, the air becoming super-heated from the explosions.

My God, this is it; it's been five years and I'm in the war; I'm in the damned war, raced through my head. Not all the training in the world can truly prepare you for that first moment of realization. My life, all my men's lives, were on the line. All this passed through my head in less than a second, and then I made sure all of the men were off the boat and shouted, as loudly as I could to make myself heard over the shelling, *"Run! Move! Move!"* We pounded through the sand, but it was deep and thick, the worst possible surface to try and make our way through quickly. It was like slogging through snow. And because it was seven-thirty in the morning by that point, we were absolutely perfect targets in the new daylight.

We covered seventy-five yards, and it felt like seventy-five hundred. Tracer bullets blew past us, in front and behind, as the Germans returned fire. The shelling from the boats hadn't been tremendously successful in actually destroying the German encampments. At best, it had bought us some time to get a toehold on the beach, but now the Germans were doing their level best to blow our toes off. Something like twelve hundred rounds a minute hurtled around us. It was as if we were wading through a swarm of infuriated hornets, hurling ourselves into the midst of an angry nest. But for all the targets that our easily visible bodies presented, my troop got off miraculously lucky. Not one of my thirty-three men was hit. It's possible that the Germans were so thrown off, so flustered by the invasion strike, that they simply didn't know where to shoot first. It was an indecision that benefited my men, although others wouldn't be quite so lucky.

The Regina Rifles weren't quite so lucky. They made it to Juno Beach, but not intact. Three of their LCAs went down— either tipping over in the waves or being blown up by one of the mines in the hedgerows. The men aboard were killed, within sight of their destination. What a waste . . . What a damned waste.

As we kept moving, we were utterly focused on our job. It was hard not to be: each soldier knew what was happening perhaps ten feet from him, and that was it. Each person knew exactly what he was supposed to do and nothing else.

Sand flew around us, bullets chewing up the beach, and then we made it to the cover of the sand dunes. My heart was pounding, my lungs slamming against my chest. I glanced back at the distance that we had covered and somehow still couldn't believe it.

We caught our breath for a moment, steeled ourselves for what further had to be done, and then bolted for a small road that would take us further inland. There we came upon Waldie and Brownridge, who were dealing with an infantry captain who had more or less come unglued. Useless to his men, the pressure and strain of the landing had discombobulated him. It was a pitiable situation, really. I'm sure that he went into the situation with as much determination and certainty in his own abilities as I had. As anyone had. But a man never knows how he's going to deal with a life-and-death situation until he finds himself faced with it, and it's at times such as those that you can learn some very unpleasant truths about yourself.

We tried to talk the captain "down" by going over what needed to be done. It seemed to settle him a bit, but we really didn't have a great deal of time to devote to him. Machine guns, explosions, we could hear it all, everything going on around us.

My assistant, Chevalier, and I took the left side of the road, and my troop, along with Waldie's and Brownridge's troops, moved forward infantry style, moving in leaps and bounds and guarding each other's back. Waldie and Brownridge went to the right side. Chevalier had the rifle, and I was armed with a 9mm automatic in addition to the Smith and Wesson from Bill.

For a brief time there was silence, and then all of a sudden machine gun fire opened up. We scrambled for cover, and as I looked around with binoculars, I located the source—a church tower about a hundred yards away. I could see, through the binoculars, two Germans in the tower. I realized they hadn't been firing at us specifically, because they were repositioning the machine gun and firing in another direction at that point. Nevertheless, they might spot us and make us their primary target, or they might pick off others on the beach.

"Take a shot at them," I said to Chevalier. "I'll watch through the binoculars."

He took aim and squeezed off a shot. Squinting through the binoculars, I saw no reaction whatsoever. They probably never even knew they'd been fired at.

I glanced at the rifle and recognized the serial number. I'd been practicing with it the week before. I knew how it fired and knew that you could hit a target at fifteen hundred yards with it, not to mention one hundred. "You take the glasses and I'll take the rifle," I said.

I'd never shot at a living being before, but it was the job. You had to do the job. I swear to you, you never thought of anything other than getting the job done. I fired off a first shot, a clean miss, but with my second shot, one of the Germans went down. I fired again immediately, and the second fell.

Slowly I lowered the rifle. Had I . . . killed them? Or just wounded them? We watched carefully for a moment, but there was no sign of movement in the tower. Whether they were alive or dead, at least the machine guns had been silenced.

We kept on moving through the little town of Graye sur Mer. We saw the French people of the village peeking out, and I knew they were the residents, not Germans. We went on through, made a left turn, and found a nice big field right next to a main road. It had enormous shell holes—fourteen-inch-gun shell holes—inverted cone-shaped holes, fifteen feet deep. We surveyed the gun positions, decided where our command post should be (namely in one of the shell holes), and waited in the warm sun. The guns were supposed to come in by ten hundred hours, and it was zero nine hundred at that point.

The infantry started to move in, the Canadian division infantry. And then we heard music, the music of bagpipes floating across the land to us. It was such a contradictory moment; there, in the midst of a war, bagpipes were playing a proud tune. It was the Fifty-first Highlanders, marching along as cheerfully and proudly as if they were on a school outing. They were all in battle dress, of course, except the bagpipers, who were in kilts. It was a proud Scots moment of tradition: centuries might have passed, the ways of war passing from sword to gunfire, yet here was the classic Scots manner of entering war passing pridefully before us, just as it had for hundreds of years. Montgomery Scott would have been proud.

It got to about ten-fifteen, and a lot of the infantry was overdue. I turned to Waldie—a big fellow, about six foot three—and said, "What do you think? Maybe we should go back to the beach and see what's happening." Finding our way wouldn't be difficult, for the main road led back down there.

We went down to the beachhead, and we could see the bottleneck was a bunch of tanks that had hit the mines and were stopped dead. The road had been blocked, and equipment was piling up on the beach like you wouldn't believe. I said to Waldie, "This looks like a dive-bomb target to me; let's get out of here," thinking of the Stukas that I had seen. Waldie readily agreed.

What we didn't know was that the Spitfires and American fighters, now that the fog had lifted, were thick in the skies, making sure that no German planes could penetrate the area.

That's where I saw my first badly wounded person. The poor bastard was sitting down with his back against a bank of soil. His whole stomach had been split open; his entrails were spilling out. He was quite alive and so doped up on morphine that he wasn't writhing in agony. They had no means of getting him anywhere, for no hospital ship was ready at the time.

He didn't even notice us. He just sat there, staring straight ahead, the stink of imminent death hanging over him. We just looked at him and then looked away.

It could have been me.

I had thought about that aspect of war, I guess, but it hadn't been paramount in my mind, to think of wounded people. When faced with moments such as that, though, you have to force yourself to feel nothing. Shut it off. But I remember it so vividly today.

We headed back and, on the way, ran into a scrappy gun position officer I knew named Tommy O'Brennan. I spotted him from a distance because he walked like the scrapper that he was, with his arms up and swinging, as if he were throwing punches with every step. When we were in Bournmouth, he'd get so drunk that he'd haul off and slug whoever was next to him. Colonel or general, it didn't matter, he'd deck you.

O'Brennan, the classic feisty, red-haired Irishman, had been on an LCA that had run into mechanical difficulties and was returning to the troop ship. They couldn't land. O'Brennan wouldn't have any of that and said to the trooper leader, "I'm jumping overboard to go and see Mr. Doohan." Which was exactly what he did. Tommy O'Brennan stormed Juno Beach singlehandedly.

We didn't fire any guns that day. Just established our position, as Field Marshal Montgomery had told us to do. War films give you the impression that a war is constant battles and skirmishes every step of the way, but it's really very much the luck of the draw. While one troop can be standing or sitting around, in what seems the most peaceful of areas, another can find themselves in a bloody, blistering battle that involves fighting for every foot of ground (as happened, for instance, at Omaha Beach).

We hunkered down and prepared to wait matters out, secure in our position and certain that the Germans would try and challenge it. We had been warned by regimental headquarters that we had not captured all the Germans between the beach and our position. A lot of them were trying to come back through our lines to reestablish their own positions.

At about eleven-thirty that night, I was walking back to my command post from another command post, with Tommy O'Brennan on my right, about a foot and a half away. We were walking around a large shell hole . . .

And that was when the machine gun opened up on us.

It hit me and spun me around. Staggering, I fell down into the shell hole. Tommy hadn't been hit at all, and for a moment I hadn't fully registered that I'd been struck. I just knew that something had shoved me with tremendous force.

Then I looked at my right hand and saw the blood covering it. I could see the holes in my middle finger.

Tommy leaped down into the shell hole with me, yanked out a grenade, pulled the pin, and then hurled it in the general direction that he was sure the machine gun had fired from. I don't know if he hit anybody; I don't think so, because we never found any bodies in the immediate area.

Staring at my perforated finger, I felt no pain. The adrenaline got in there and acted as a buffer, although I knew I'd feel it later. I felt as if I were looking at it from a distance, as if it had happened to someone else.

My training kicked in as sort of an autopilot, I said, "I'd better get to the regimental post and get this fixed." I sounded amazingly calm. I was probably slightly in shock, although to be utterly sanguine about it, one has to remember that it's one of the natural consequences of war. *Somebody's* got to get shot. There was even *some* humor to the situation, in that I could tell from Tommy's expression that he was damned glad it hadn't been him. Tommy wound up taking over my troop, which included my tank, with my bedroll stuffed with my 3,600 British pounds of craps winnings. The tank was blown up on June 7, before Tommy ever found the money. Easy come, easy go.

(As it turned out, that unhappy moment in Normandy was the last time I ever saw him. He went on to become an air observation pilot (AOP) and then died some years later in a plane crash in Toronto, in 1957. I remember sitting there watching a report of it on the news, wondering if he'd been drinking.)

I walked to the regimental aid post, which, like everything else, was situated in a shell hole. I presented my hand, looking at it with a kind of bemusement as the medic bandaged it up. Somehow I wasn't focusing on this as anything other than a temporary inconvenience. I figured they'd patch me up, and I'd head right back to my men.

Judging by the bullet holes, three bullets had struck the finger. The medic finished bandaging my hand, and I started to get up to leave. But he said to me in confusion, "Now, what about your leg?"

I looked down. *My leg?* I hadn't been shot in the leg. I'd walked over to the aid post with no difficulty, not so much as a limp.

But, sure enough, my left knee was covered with blood. The medic tore the pant leg off from the thigh down and said, "See? You were hit here, too."

Damned if I hadn't been. I couldn't believe it. I'd taken a bullet in the leg as well. Then my astonishment grew as he removed bullet after bullet . . . two, three, then a fourth.

I looked away from the damaged leg, wanting to look anywhere else. And as I glanced down at my shirt, I noticed something.

The upper right pocket of the shirt was torn. In the upper right corner, there was one, possibly two, bullet holes.

I'd been shot in the chest.

My mind was trying to make sense of it. Four bullets in the leg, and I was still walking. Amazing. But a bullet in the chest, square into my lungs, and I was still breathing with no sign of distress? Impossible.

But there was the bullet hole.

Trembling, I reached across with my left hand to the right shirt pocket. I don't think the medic even noticed, because he was busy with the leg.

I pulled out the sterling silver cigarette case that my brother

Bill had given me when I was his best man. And there I discovered a dent in it.

The bullet had come in at an angle, ricocheted off the cigarette case, and bounced away. Four inches from my heart.

Can you imagine that in an episode of *Star Trek?* Scotty's life saved because a stray phaser blast was deflected by a silver cigarette case given him by his brother. Fans would shake their heads and think that the writers had lost their minds, falling back on unlikely clichés. "His brother saved his life from thousands of miles away! Boy, that's pushing it!"

The landing ship that had been converted into an ambulance was enormous, with soldiers stacked ten, fifteen bunks high. The medics were like Tarzan, swinging from one bunk to the other. As I lay there, bandaged and bewildered, a medic would sweep into view, say, "You okay?" When getting the affirmative response, he'd hop off to someone else, giving him morphine for the pain, marking his forehead to indicate the number of doses he'd received.

By eleven the next morning I was in an English hospital in Basingstoke, a south-coast town about thirty miles inland, where the first wounded were being brought in. All around me, men were sleeping or moaning softly, and a few sobs of pain or frustration would float over to me. There was nothing to take our attention away from the agony and anguish we were experiencing—the agony of the wounds, and the anguish that we had been taken out so early in the game.

How much more frustration would we have felt, I wonder, had we heard the Germans reporting defiantly that the Normandy invasion had been a spectacular failure. Not surprising, really. What else were they going to say? "The Allies suckered us completely"?

The medics pumped me with sedatives to calm me down, because the shock of what had happened was wearing off and the full realization was settling in. Once I'd been calmed down, the surgeons—who were operating on a brutal schedule of forty-eight hours on, twelve off, forty-eight hours on—

operated on me without even bothering with X rays. They clipped off the top of the finger, down to the first knuckle, but that was all. Further decisions would wait until after it had been X-rayed.

A day later I was sent to a Canadian hospital, built on Lady Astor's estate, Cliveden. I was operated on again, just to check everything. It was at that point that they took the X rays. Up until then, I was hoping that there was a good chance of recovery, that I would be able to make use of the rest of the finger again once it had recovered.

But the X rays weren't promising. They indicated that the bones had been shattered.

The third day after the invasion, there were lists of wounded put into the papers. The Sarnia newspaper, *The Observer,* had a picture of me in my officer's uniform, saying "Sarnia wounded," describing me and reporting that I had been wounded during the D day landing. My poor folks, getting word of it in that fashion. Still, at least I was listed among "wounded" rather than "deceased."

I stayed in the hospital for a time, recovering, with sulfa drugs on my knee to prevent infection. Then, after several weeks, I was moved to a convalescent hospital in Colchester, where they checked the finger and took more X rays, wondering what they should do about it. Finally they sat me down and said, "Look, the most reasonable option is to amputate the rest of the finger." I think I must have gone a little white. "Otherwise," they continued, "it's going to remain stiff for the rest of your life. The bones are shattered; there's nothing we can do to salvage them." Ultimately, the decision was up to me, and it was truly a hellish choice. Either be minus a finger on my right hand, or spend my life looking as though I was flipping someone an obscene gesture any time I relaxed the other fingers of the hand.

I went to a pub in town, trying to sort things out. And darned if I didn't meet the film actor Van Heflin there. I'd always been impressed by Van Heflin, who starred in such films as *Grand Central Murder,* and would go on to star in such noted films as *Shane.* He was in the U.S. Army Corps. I'd love to be able to say that there was a man who epitomized my two dreams, aviation and acting. But in fact I had no real aspirations toward acting, and at the time I was more concerned about such earthbound crises as what to do about my finger. Still, he came across as a regular, nice kind of guy.

Later, as I got on a big, double-decker bus, the first thing I saw was a guy with that finger missing. I tried not to look as if I was staring at him, and I don't know how successful I was. Ultimately, though, I said, *"Hmm,* well . . . that doesn't look so bad."

I got off the bus, went back to the doctors, and said, "Okay, we'll operate on Monday."

And on Monday, they doped me up with sodium pentothal for an anesthetic. People think it's a truth serum, but it's not exactly. What it does is knock out your inhibitions.

So there I was, in a room with about twenty other wounded guys, and I was in a bizarre state that combined both nervousness and giddiness. A nurse sat down next to me, talking to me soothingly, holding my hand.

And I, high as a kite, reached over and held her. . . .

Well, let's say that she just took it in stride, and the other guys were all jealous.

8

Junior Birdman

THERE'S NOTHING LIKE GETTING A DEAR JOHN LETTER FIVE WEEKS after you've had your finger blown off to put spring in a man's stride.

I had returned to Camp Borden and was given mail that should have, by rights, gotten to me before D day. But because we had been in a variety of training camps, the mail had just followed me from army post office to army post office, always one step behind me.

And there was the letter from Kay Glynn, nine pages in which she was trying to explain the entire situation to me.

She had hooked up with a doctor, Joe Cherry, whom she had met at McGill University. He was from Danbury, Connecticut, having come up to be trained in Canada.

She had chosen a course in her life, and there was I, in the army for the run of the war, which had gone on year after year, five damn years and still counting. Despite the German claims that D day had been a debacle, we knew that it had been a resounding success. For our part, twenty-five thousand Canadians had participated. Of that number, we'd lost a little over a thousand men. We'd taken a bite out of the Germans and participated in an operation that was the first major step in taking back occupied Europe.

But none of that meant we were going home anytime soon. And even if I'd been on the next flight out, I would be . . . what? Running back to unemployment? Still with no direction in life? What the hell did I have to offer to Glynn? Glynn, who had waited five years. Oh, sure, we had discussed her waiting for me, but who knew that it would be so long? And who knew how much longer it would be?

There was nothing I could do, nothing anyone could say. For so long, it had just been a sort of "given" that Glynn and I would be married. With the loss of that constant in my life, it brought home with ugly force just how little I had to look forward to when I returned. Whenever my army stint did end, I was going to be dropped right back into the situation I'd come to consider a distant memory.

Feeling at a loss, feeling empty inside, I took the letter to the general in charge. He read it and said, "Oh, God, I've got to send you home."

I could see in his face that from the familiar, intimate way that Glynn had written to me, it had come across as if she were my wife, leaving me for another man. "We're not married, sir," I informed him.

"Oh." Then he took me out into his garden, with his hand on my shoulder, and he said all the things one is supposed to say at that time—*that there'd be another streetcar coming along eventually.* (In looking back, considering that I'd marry three times, I was a damned streetcar terminal.) The truth was, I needed something besides that talk, some sort of answers to all the questions that were tumbling around in me. But I couldn't articulate the questions, and even if I could have, he certainly wouldn't have known what to tell me. Nevertheless, the talk was great, and he was a terrific guy.

But I needed something else. Some other form of escape, something else to look toward.

I walked back to the headquarters, looking at the skies, while my footsteps felt heavy as lead. And then, right there on the bulletin board at HQ, was a notice advertising for artillery officers who wanted to volunteer for air observation.

Air observation.

All the old feelings of escape, of leaving the earth and its problems behind, came back to me with dizzying speed. It was remarkable. Minutes earlier I had felt heavy, laden down . . . and now I was almost giddy with anticipation.

And I said to no one in particular, except perhaps the divine providence that had tossed this opportunity in front of me, "They're going to teach me to fly."

Elementary Flight Training School (EFTS) was in Cambridge, about fifty miles northeast of London. I had a little apartment in a small town called Cherry Hinton, where I acquired a considerable reputation as a player of a local game called shove ha'penny. I beat old fellows there who'd been playing it for forty years.

My flight instructor was a sergeant in the Royal Air Force. As I climbed into the plane for my first flight, my heart was racing and it was all I could do to listen to his instructions about where all the straps, buckles, and belts snapped together.

It was a Tiger Moth biplane, a very old aircraft but a damned good one—open-air cockpit and everything. The planes you see in Red Baron movies are modified Tiger Moths with slightly altered noses. I'd love to have one today.

We took off, my flight instructor at the controls, and I looked down as the ground dropped away from me. I would love to tell you that this was a moment of euphoria for me, the realization of a lifelong dream.

Instead, sudden anxiety cramped up my insides. Remember, despite the fascination and allure flight had had for me, I had never been in a plane before. I swear, if I'd been able to ditch the harness quickly, I'd have jumped out.

But once we got above a hundred and fifty feet, the ground didn't seem to be moving away quite so quickly, and I never again got that panicked feeling of wanting to bolt the plane.

The plane was loud as anything, and it would have been impossible to hear anything the flight instructor said if it hadn't been for a bizarre speaker device, a sort of tubelike rig that ran from one cockpit to the next. And the instructor said, "Do you want to take control?"

My first thought was *Already?* Gamely, I took over the controls, but I wouldn't exactly say I was "in control." We wavered over the airspace quite a bit, because I really wasn't sure of what I was supposed to be doing.

I logged seven and a half hours before I was ready to go solo, which was about average for trainees. (If you were at it longer than ten and no one had faith in you to bring the plane back in one piece, you pretty much wiped out of the program.) Once I was soloing, though, I logged ninety-three hours in the period of time that it took other fellows to rack up forty-five.

During one of my first solo spins, I was climbing higher and higher, then looking down and back because I was going to make a left turn. And there, a thousand feet below me, was a huge Lancaster four-engine bomber, obviously out on maneuvers. And apparently the pilot decided to have some "fun," because it came right at me.

I made a sharp left, and it came up high on my right. It was banking around, clearly about to come at me again. I wagged my wings, which is the signal that you're a student. The bomber dove underneath me and then came up in front again, and somebody in the tail was waving at me.

Funny guys.

Not quite as funny, though, as the time I did my first cross-country and damn near collided with a twin-engine bomber. I was at two thousand feet, checking my compass, and suddenly the bomber was coming right at me. I think we spotted each other at exactly the same moment, because we both swerved at the same time to avoid collision. His left wingtip was just five feet away from my wheels as I turned.

Another time I was cruising along at ten thousand feet, feeling fairly confident. Then I heard the air around me start to come alive, as if a massive swarm of bees were heading my way. The plane began to vibrate in response, and then I saw them coming—an entire wing of B-17s, thirty-seven planes. I had gotten out of the way and figured that I was in the clear, when suddenly I got caught in the prop wash. When we're speaking of the prop wash of thirty-seven planes, we're talking about being tossed around like a bloody feather. You get 148 engines going and it's something else. I didn't recover from that until I was down to about five thousand feet.

But for every death-defying problem I encountered, there was also an interesting . . . "perk." For example, I'd land in a farmer's field, taxi over to the farmhouse, get out, get a couple of dozen eggs from the farmer's wife, and take off again. The next morning the cook would produce fresh eggs for breakfast.

But I was never able to lose sight of the fact that there was a war going on. At certain times in the afternoon, while I was up and about, training, I'd have to be watchful for B-17s and P-50s coming back from bombing missions. I'd see bombers with ten or twelve feet of fuselage just ripped off; I'd see gun turrets dangling with nobody in them. Planes would come limping in, sometimes flying on two engines, with maybe one engine hanging off the wing. They were trying to make it back to their fields, and some of them looked like they would never get there.

Once again, just as had happened so many other times in my life, I was put in positions where I had to prove myself. There was one instructor, an Englishman who had been trained near Calgary, who just took a flat-out dislike to me (and I admit I was none-too-thrilled with him). We had to practice pinpoint landings, coming down on a large letter *T* laid out in white cloth.

The instructor was making me so nervous that I would float and go twenty feet too short or too far. He got snotty with me and said, "Well, it sure doesn't look as if you can handle this."

And I just lost my temper and snapped, "If you'd get the hell out of here, I'd handle it just fine. I'll land within inches of it instead of twenty feet, because the only problem I'm having trouble with is *you.*"

My outburst was enough to convince him that I couldn't possibly handle the landing, and he was more than happy to clear out so I'd have no "excuse." He stood off about fifteen or twenty yards. I took off and came in five times, and every time I was within five inches of the spot.

"Okay," I said, probably more smugly than was wise, "does that satisfy you?"

He said, "Okay," albeit reluctantly. That was the last time I had to deal with that particular instructor.

From there I graduated to the Mark-5 observer planes. If the Tiger Moth biplanes were something that Snoopy would have flown, the Mark-5 might have been a cousin to Wonder Woman's "invisible plane." The plane had Plexiglas right down to the tail, big windows, and windshield. The only real protection we had was learning how to fly low, because we had no armor plate behind us to stop bullets. We had no machine guns, nothing to fire unless we opened a window, took out a pistol, and started shooting.

I had an English instructor—renowned for his command of dirty English sex songs—who kept prodding me to take more and more chances in my low flying. He even called me chicken, and I said to him, "That's enough of that 'chicken' stuff." So the very next time I went out, I not only buzzed Stonehenge, but I played tag with an American convoy on the road, touching my wheels down between each vehicle before slaloming between them with my wing about six inches off the road. When I related that little excursion to the English instructor, he said, "By God, you're no longer chicken, are you!" He was rather jolly with me, after that. I doubt he'd ever done anything like that himself.

That was really what flying was all about to me. Pushing myself, challenging myself, not having any trepidation about taking on new tests. If the liberating feeling of flying meant anything, it meant liberating myself from those fears that could hold me back.

Brigadier General Ziegler was not my biggest fan.

Actually, he'd once been ready to court-martial me. Back before D day, when he was Colonel Ziegler, I'd refused to obey orders he'd given during an artillery practice. My rationale seemed reasonable to me at the time; I knew if I did what he ordered, I would have wound up blowing the heads off some of my men. It hadn't seemed worth decapitating some good soldiers simply to honor the chain of command. Ziegler had wanted me arrested on the spot, and only some very fast talking from my superior officers had prevented me from being court-martialed.

So here it was, May of 1945, and I had been stationed at a place called Dordrecht, in Holland. I was informed that I was to fly Brigadier General Ziegler over to the headquarters of Field Marshal Montgomery in Bad Oeynhausen, Germany, which was about 120 miles northeast of Dordrecht. Indeed, Ziegler had been on the phone with my brother (who was a full colonel by that point) and said, "Yes, your young brother's going to be flying me to Bad Oeynhausen, and I don't want *any* problems with him this time."

Ziegler arrived about a quarter to seven in the morning. He was wearing a uniform that must have cost him plenty, because it fit him extremely well and he weighed about 280 pounds. He also had two big briefcases with him, each about forty pounds, and I knew immediately we were going to have a problem. With all the weight he was packing, so to speak, I didn't have enough runway to get off the ground. We were in a quarter-mile circle, ringed in by fences.

Immediately I waved over the flight mechanics. "Quick," I said, "go get some help. Take out that fence, and that fence over there, move them back. Then smooth that ground out." I glanced over my shoulder at Ziegler, who was already looking impatient. "I'll take him in for a cup of coffee, and when you guys are ready, you tell me."

I went back to him and, trying to sound casual, I said, "Sir, we're not quite ready yet." He wore his annoyance like a shroud around himself, but what was I supposed to tell him? That he was too damn heavy to get off the ground easily? He'd probably blame it on me somehow.

When we were ready to take off, I told the mechanics, "For God's sake, don't let him see you—but I want you to take the tail and push, so I can get a good start." I figured I'd need all the help I could get.

Even with the fences pushed back, we just barely cleared them, and even then I had to use an emergency flap to get over the hump and then had to dodge a group of trees.

He had to do the map reading to get to Bad Oeynhausen. There was no prepared runway there yet, and we had a heck of a time finding the field. All of a sudden, as I was curving off in the other direction, I suddenly spotted four small planes under trees, and a car waiting for Ziegler at the gate. I just said, "Here we go, sir," and did a steep turn and landed, pulling right up to the car. I leaped out and got him out of the plane, and he looked at me unevenly—a little shaky, I think, from the sharp angling and abrupt landing. "Boy, I don't know about you, Doohan. I just don't know about you at all."

And I said, "Well, sir, we're here safely."

"Yes, thank God," he answered.

I had a similar, rather bizarre experience with a medical colonel, shortly after V-E Day. He really didn't know anything about the army. They didn't give those guys a course; they just gave them a uniform and had them run hospitals, like on *M*A*S*H*. I had to take him to Detmold, Germany.

We were flying along, and I didn't seem to be passing over

anything that he recognized. And he said, "Do you know where we're going?"

I said, "Certainly, sir."

Ten minutes went by, and he was getting nervous, because I was only two hundred feet above ground. Trying to catch me, he suddenly said challengingly, "What's the name of that little town there?"

Without hesitation, I said briskly, "That's Brittenhausen." In fact, I had no idea what it was. I just made up the German name.

"Oh. Okay." But he was still suspicious, and he said, "Show me that on the map."

Trying to sound impatient rather than caught in a lie, I said, "Sir, I have to fly. Can't *you* find it?"

"No, I can't," he said tartly.

I knew the autobahn was coming up, so I said, "To let you know where we are, we'll be crossing the autobahn pretty soon, and then we'll go to the left." He scanned the ground nervously, and I could almost sense him relaxing when the autobahn came into view. "Oh, you *do* know where you're going, don't you?" he said, sounding relieved.

One time, flying over Germany again, I stalled out at about one hundred and fifty feet. I wound up landing on the autobahn, turned the prop . . . and it worked. I got back in and took off down the autobahn.

At the first *Star Trek* convention I attended in Nuremberg, I told that story and a fellow said, "My father saw that! He saw a small aircraft land across the autobahn, and he was so amazed."

May 7 of 1945 brought V-E Day . . . Victory in Europe day. It was a tremendous relief, and we were absolutely filled with joy that we had defeated the Germans. I was in Amsterdam at the time, and I remember driving my jeep and doing wheelies around the bomb holes on the road.

The unconditional German surrender brought a time of

international euphoria. There was celebration throughout Canada, a sense of national pride that their six-year contribution of brave and valiant Canadians had aided in the downfall of a terrible evil. Keep in mind that even though we had been beating Hitler back and it seemed as if the Third Reich was crumbling, one never truly *knew* for sure what was going to happen. It had been as if we were holding our collective breath for half a decade, and when the Germans gave up, it was as if there was a global exhalation (and I can assure you that a good deal of that breath was scented with celebrational spirits that day).

At that point, I was faced with the prospect of going home. That's what we all figured, in any event. And there I was, anticipating a homecoming that involved no job, no career path, and matters that were still unsettled with my father. God, I'd been a soldier, faced bullets, and seen death. Was I supposed to go back to being the scared little boy?

But then the Japanese made it clear that they were not going to fall in line behind the crumbling Axis powers, and that they would continue the war. The call went out for volunteers to go to Florida or San Diego to train in taking off and landing on a landing ship. It was that particularly difficult sort of landing that I'm sure you've seen in many an aviator movie, where one has to come in at just the right height and speed to hook onto a wire that will bring you to a halt. Time it wrong, miss the wire, and you and your entire plane go straight into the ocean.

More death-defying risks? Well . . . it beat facing down my dad. So off to San Diego I would go, practicing takeoffs and landings and anticipating being called into service in the battle against Japan.

I was perfectly willing to be patient. Keep in mind they'd had us training for *five years* before I saw my first major action. So being kept on station for four months in San Diego was hardly what I would call a hardship.

And, as it turned out, it only took four months, because Harry Truman dropped two atomic bombs on the Japanese, on August 6 and 9, and that was the end of the war. It's become popular nowadays to second-guess Truman's decision, but all I can tell you is that, while we were willing to fight on for however long it took, no one was breathless with anticipation over continuing the war for year after year. The bomb ended the war. Unfortunately it also ended the lives of thousands of Japanese souls. Truman never wavered on the rightness of his action, and speaking as a possible beneficiary of his decision, I feel it was nice to have made it through the war . . . if not in one piece, then in a condition fairly close to it. Still, I'd be very surprised if the imagined screams of those thousands who died in the nuclear holocaust of Hiroshima and Nagasaki didn't haunt Truman in his private hours.

As for me, even though I was going home instead of to the Pacific, I had regrets about my aborted flying career. At night, while waiting for my marching orders home, I'd dream about flying over the Blue Water Bridge between Port Huron and Sarnia, doing a loop around it. In later years I would fly from time to time—rented a plane in Toronto a couple of times. And just a couple of years ago I was on a cruise and took over the controls of a seaplane.

The problem is, I never even got an official pilot's license. Still, maybe I'll do it sometime. Where I live now, in Washington State, there's plenty of water around, and there are lakes in British Columbia as well, so I'd love to take a seaplane and do some puddle jumping—and then head for the skies, because, no matter how old I get, there's still that need to leave the earth behind. And without a starship at my beck and call, I'll have to take what I can get.

9

How You Gonna Keep 'Em Down on the Farm . . . ?

SINCE THE ARMY DOESN'T DO ANYTHING IN A STRAIGHTFORWARD manner if a roundabout way exists, I was not sent from the relative closeness of San Diego straight up to Sarnia. Instead, I was shipped back to England . . . then to Holland . . . then back to England (missing the troop train that was bound for there, I wound up stealing a jeep in order to make the ferry), from there we boarded a French passenger liner. The ocean voyage there was the polar opposite of the trip to Europe, choppy and fierce with not a wave that was under thirty feet. Go figure—smooth sailing heading into war, rough going during peacetime.

We came into Montreal, and that was the first chance I'd had to phone my family. I got my sister on the phone. I said, "Margaret?"

She said, "Yes?"

I barely recognized her voice. It had been six years, and I can only imagine what I sounded like to her, but to me her voice sounded harsh, almost nasal. It was a shocker after six years of listening to the relative softness of Englishwomen's voices. *"Jimmy, is that you?! How are you!!?"*

"Margaret?" I said, trying to hide my incredulity.

"Yeah!" She probably thought I couldn't believe I was hearing her voice, and she was right, but not for the reason she thought.

I didn't say anything to her, of course. What could I say? "Boy, sis, I never realized what a jolting voice you have." So naturally, I didn't say anything. It didn't take me long to realize that my mother likewise had a strong accent, although hardly as nasal and jarring as Margaret's.

When she found out it was me, she cried because she was so happy to have me home. As for me, I was still racked with uncertainty as to what I was going to do with my life now. The Great Depression was over, but I was still unemployed, with no clear sense of what I wanted to do to earn a living. Nevertheless, I felt I could put all those concerns aside for the moment and just embrace the joy of being reunited with my family.

It took me another twenty hours to get home, arriving at the train station and from there being transported to my house by the army. I know my family would have met me at the train station if it had been at all possible, but unfortunately it wasn't, because my mother was having extreme trouble walking. Arthritis had taken a terrible toll on her and would become even more pronounced in the future. But for once, the future wasn't hanging over me. Instead, I just hugged her for at least five minutes. I don't remember much of what was said; perhaps nothing was. Perhaps it was one of those times where nothing needed to be said.

They looked over my hand where the finger had been removed. My family was pretty much an unshockable bunch (steeling oneself to live with my father did that for you), and instead of being appalled, they commented admiringly on the surgery. "Oh, that's a neat job," they said.

And as for my father . . .

I was still carrying all the resentment toward him that was eating away at the basis of our relationship like root rot. But this was not the time to vent my frustration, because he was making it clear that he was very proud of the service to our country that both Bill and I had provided. I know he was jealous of us, having served our country in a way that he'd never been able to, but at least he didn't make an open display of that envy.

And besides, I probably caught him flat-footed when I suddenly opined that I could do with a shot of scotch and said, "How about you, Dad? Care for a drink?" He put on a great air of bluster, of "Oh, ha, well, okay, if you *insist,"* as if he'd never had a drink in his life. The very fact that he was having a social drink with his children really threw him. He didn't know what to say. That was unusual.

It had been a year since I'd gotten Kay's Dear John letter. The resentment and stinging hurt I'd felt at the time had long passed. I'd kept no ill feeling because I felt I really couldn't hold her to her intention to wait for me.

But with peace declared and my having returned home, it seemed like a good opportunity to get together again. So I called her up and we had a date. I took her over to Port Huron for dinner and dancing. We danced to a song by Perry Como called " 'Til the End of Time." That was "our song," as of that time, or as of that night, at any rate.

The evening was certainly wonderful, but I knew that Kay was already set in her relationship with Joe Cherry. He had so much to offer her, and I had nothing, really. I was certain that she was just seeing me out of a sense of loyalty to what we had once had, and I was more than willing to take it on that basis.

I didn't realize that my assessment of the situation was 180 degrees wrong and, in fact, wouldn't learn that until about four decades later.

What was accurate, though, was my awareness that I had nothing planned for myself. One day I was talking to my brother Bill. I had saved about $3,500 by sending half my pay home and living on the other half. He suggested I go to the Veterans Administration school to bone up on subjects that I hadn't studied for nearly seven years. I said that was a great idea, moved to London, Ontario, and started going to veterans school. Nonetheless, I was twenty-six years old and still had no career in mind, although I was dabbling with the thought of getting into chemistry.

At the very end of the year, sometime around Christmas of 1945, it was a Thursday night around eight P.M. I stopped studying, turned on the radio, and listened to a drama show that had just come on. It was the worst damn radio show I had ever heard. I couldn't believe how bad it was. I asked the otherwise empty room, "Is this amateur night for actors or something?"

I had no idea where the show was broadcast from, whether it was from the United States or Canada. I turned the damn thing off and went to get some stuff to read. But not to read to myself, to read out loud. Rather than being seized with any sort of acting bug, my thinking was more along the lines of frustration with inadequacy. After all, I'd spent six years in the army, working under officers who were determined to shape me into the best soldier I could be and, in turn, training other men to achieve their own potential. So to be listening to the radio and hearing substandard work, well . . . it just rubbed me the wrong way.

I went down to CFPL, a radio station, the next morning and said, "I want to make a recording."

"Well, we call them transcriptions," the technician said.

"I don't care. I want to make one. How much does it cost?" He told me, and I paid that. I recorded some Shakespeare and some books on philosophy, and then I listened to it. I cringed, having never heard my own voice before. I said, "God, that's awful!"

"What the hell are you talking about?" said the technician. "That's good!"

Interesting how directions in one's life take a turn. If the technician had agreed with me, for all I know I might have skulked away and that would have been that. Instead, armed with that praise, I said, "Where do you go to learn how to act?"

If God was plotting my life for me, he was dropping in plot twists in rather obvious fashion. "Strange that you should ask," the technician said. "A brochure just arrived about an hour ago in the mail from a drama school in Toronto. Why don't you check it out?"

I read the brochure from the Academy of Radio Arts and sent them a telegram. A couple of hours later I got an answer back. And I was there on Sunday night—school started on Monday—got a room in a rooming house way out in Eglinton. Six months later, I had won the top scholarship, two years of free tuition at the Neighborhood Playhouse in New York City. I didn't know it, but at the time that was the best school in the country.

During that summer, from June until the middle of September, I had preparations to make. I went around getting a student green card and had to find some distant cousins in the States—they turned out to be in Brooklyn—to put me up. They were lovely people, a married couple with terrific singing voices.

I also took the time to see John Gielgud in *The Importance of Being Earnest.* Knowing that I would shortly be endeavoring to follow that path, I watched him with an appraising eye that I might not have directed toward him before. He is, in my opinion, the greatest actor in the world. Either he has incredible instincts or he does meticulous preparation—or both—because I've never seen him make an acting misstep, and I can't say that about any other actor.

Sometime later I'd see him again, in *Medea* with Judith Anderson. I was up in the cheap seats at a point in the play where Judith Anderson asks him a question. With his back solidly to the audience, he replies, *"No!"* and I could hear it resonate all the way up to where I was sitting. Now, *that* was quality voice production, and achieved with apparently no effort at all.

My mother never said anything about my intended vocation other than, "Whatever it is, that's fine." My father, on the other hand, said to Bill, "What the hell's he doing, going in to be an actor?!"

Bill said to him, "You just leave him alone. He knows what he's doing." Which, of course, I didn't think I knew at all. I had no idea what I was doing.

But as my life was preparing to go in one direction, my parents were going in another. The arthritis took over my mother, you see. It brought her heels right up near her buttocks. She'd lie in bed like that, with her legs curled back around. I suppose it's possible that it was aggravated by the many years she'd spent using her feet to operate that sewing machine.

She went into the hospital in London, Ontario, and there she would stay for nearly nine years. She found her greatest consolation in the Catholic church. She would say the rosary, entering a state of meditative consciousness called alpha. She would sit there and say the rosary fifty, sixty times a day. During Lent, every day of the week we would all kneel down and go through the rosary. Even my father, whom I think my mother would just mentally force down to his knees.

I saw my father's lack of faith, his extreme reluctance to do anything that gave my mother any happiness. And here I was, about to move on with my life . . . except I couldn't. I felt I had tremendous unfinished business with my father, which I couldn't find a way in myself to resolve.

Yet, shortly before I left for New York to begin what would become my acting career . . . it happened. I hadn't planned it—thought about it a million times, over the course of the years, but not planned it.

At that point, late in 1946, when I finally confronted him about his drinking, I wasn't the scared little boy who'd cowered upstairs in his bedroom anymore. Nor was I the raw young man who'd joined the army to fight a hated enemy. I was grown, I'd survived a good deal, and all of a sudden I found myself going head-to-head with the man whose drinking had pervaded and overshadowed my young life.

Willie Doohan was sitting in the living room of the old house in Sarnia. As is always the case in such instances, the room seemed smaller than I'd remembered it. The furnishings in it were stuff that my mother had had to scrimp and save in order to purchase, paying out sixteen dollars a month to a furniture place called Pippins. There was never any significant contribution from my father, because half of his salary was always plowed into the alcohol.

But it wasn't just the room that seemed smaller. Somehow . . . he did, too.

I hadn't come there for the purpose of having a confrontation. It was just a visit to discuss other matters—my mother's welfare, my intended career direction. But the anger I felt toward my father was always bubbling just below the surface, and this time . . . this time . . . without my expecting it, it boiled over. Before I knew it, like a grenade, my rage exploded throughout the living room, fury hurtling in all directions like shrapnel and cutting deep, so deep.

"All the problems your drinking caused," I snapped at him. "With all the money you poured down your throat . . . God, with all that money, you could have sent Tom away to college! You could have sent Bill away! I would lie awake at night, shaking in my cot, lying there until all hours of the morning until you would settle down! Do you have any idea what that was like?"

And, of course, he did. What must have been going through his mind? The man had fled Ireland to make a better life for his children, and his own weaknesses had made it that much more difficult.

It was just the two of us in the house, just the two of us. In a way, that's how it had seemed in the past. I quavering in my bed upstairs, my father downstairs raging, and neither my mother nor my siblings could make the fear go away. Only I could.

Tears rolled down his face, but he made no sound. No sound at all. They were frozen-faced tears.

I don't remember the last thing I said to him. I don't remember the exact way the confrontation ended. All I remember is that silence, that eerie silence as my anger washed over him and he just sat there.

I felt tremendous satisfaction at the time, but it's only now, looking back, that I really regret laying into him—for two reasons. First, because it was the last time I saw him. How can it be that one tries to find closure in his life, and winds up thinking he's achieved it, only to have regrets later over how it all turned out with no way of rectifying it.

And second, because life is tough enough for a weak person like him. Even though he was supposed to be strong in every other way, he was terribly weak there.

Alcohol can be a devastating thing if you can't control it. Neither of my brothers drink much. I drink more than both of them put together, I think.

Fortunately, I have the willpower to just say, "Okay, that's it; I'm not going to do this anymore." Six or seven weeks later, I may start again. Right now, at the time of this writing, I've said to myself, "No more drinking at home; but I'll drink when I work, like going to conventions, sitting down and doing autographs." I want a double scotch there. I want two double scotches there, depending on how long I sit. I'll sit for forty minutes at a stretch and not take a drink.

I heard somebody say once that if you can go thirty-six hours without the desire to have a drink, you're not an alcoholic. I have proven that to myself so many times.

Unfortunately, for me, I'm one of those drinkers who can drink and never show anything. A great friend of mine passed away about five years ago: Ralph Thorson, who was the basis for Steve McQueen's role in his last movie, *The Hunter*. Ralph was a big man. I'd be sitting at his bar and drinking, and he'd say, "God, it's amazing. You just never seem to show it." And I said, "Yeah, I guess that's true." I think the last time I was drunk was thirty-five years ago. I just don't like being drunk.

But my father was definitely an alcoholic. He really couldn't stop it.

I suppose my relationship with my father affected the way I dealt with my own kids. I was pretty tough, also. I used to give bare-bottom spankings, but even that ended over a decade ago. I believe I regard my children far more lovingly than my father ever regarded us.

10

Treading the Boards

I went to the Neighborhood Playhouse in fear and trembling, certain that I didn't have any talent and convinced that I'd be found out in no time. I really didn't know anything about acting. Other kids would say, "I've done fifty or sixty plays." And me? I'd played Robin Hood in high school. What the hell was that? Nothing.

The Neighborhood Playhouse was situated on 54th Street between First and Second Avenues. The teacher there was a fellow named Sandy Meisner, a very funny looking guy who was about five foot five, with very thick glasses and a kind of hunched shoulder. And I swear to you, I have never found the man to be wrong. Every word that he said, boy, I swear to you, I acted upon.

I had been there less than ten days when I learned that I had to do a scene from a play of my choice. Well, I didn't know any scenes from any plays that I wanted to do. So one guy suggested we do a particular scene from Molière, and I said, "Oh, sure."

So we did the scenes at the end of the class, and when it let out, I sought out one of the senior students—a fellow named

Richard Boone who went on to no little fame himself—and said, "What's going to happen? What's he going to say to us? What will Sandy Meisner say?"

And Richard said, "Absolutely nothing. You'll never hear about it again. He just wants to see you up there on stage, doing it."

So I went to class the next morning, secure in my knowledge that there wouldn't be any commentary on the previous day's performance. And Meisner walked in, sat down, looked us all over . . . and then his gaze came to rest on me. And he said, "Well, Mr. Doohan, very funny. But now you have to learn how to *act.*" As the laughter echoed in my head, I said to myself, *"Oh God."*

Sandy Meisner was actually one of the junior members of the Group Theater. He talked to Stella Adler, who had gone over to Russia in the mid 1930s and seen Stanislavsky in action. Konstantin Stanislavsky, a Russian actor, producer, and cofounder of the Moscow Art Theater, is known as the founder of Method Acting. The Method, as it's called, is a very introspective means of acting, calling upon the actor to get inside the character's inner thoughts and feelings, often calling upon the actor's own experiences to bring authenticity to the mix.

But Sandy's views on acting were somewhat different, an alternate spin on Method that is not easy to describe. What he really taught went beyond a simple imitation of life. Rather, he raised everything up, making it more dangerous, more a "heightened reality."

Think, for instance, of my relationship with my father. It hung over me for twenty years before matters reached a head. But simply reaching into those feelings that occurred over the course of two decades wouldn't necessarily be strong enough, because one has to compress what happens within the course of twenty years into—for example—a two-hour stage piece.

Or, to put it another way: Real life doesn't always make for real drama.

Sandy started out with what he called one-action problems, wherein we would set up a scene with a specific goal that we had to imbue with our own ingenuity. For example: You want to steal something from Mary, and you happen to know how to get into her house. You have to build up a whole scene for yourself. You have to steal the object without her knowing anything about it. You have to get away without getting caught. You'd have to build the entire scene for yourself. In this way, you would create your own reality, which is the essence of acting.

I did those problems, and I said, "My God, that's as close to real as you can possibly be. If you're any closer than that, you're crazy!" In the "theft" scenario, your emotions—the fear of being caught and everything else—take on a real validity. If you believe in all of that, you're approaching the core of becoming a good actor.

It seized my imagination. I was constantly planning new scenarios, developing them in my mind, working out all the aspects. To me it was absolutely the most marvelous thing in the world. Sandy would give me horizon after horizon to reach for and keep on going.

I did a scene with another guy, and Sandy wanted us to do something else together. There was a scene called "Little Old Boy," about a couple of young fellows in the South, eleven- or twelve-year-olds. In the course of the scene, the other character dies. I walk in and there's his body. And I just threw myself on him, crying out his name, burying myself in his sweater.

But I couldn't cry. Couldn't generate any tears.

Nevertheless, I got tremendous praise from Sandy on that. And I wasn't sure why, because I still had the sense that I didn't know what I was doing. I was flying on instinct, and because I felt uneasy with my acting, I was equally uneasy with taking compliments for it. My attitude was, "What the hell? I don't understand this."

Years later, I realized why I had done it right. I had done all the tiny little actions—throwing myself on him, that was a truthful action, and burying my head in his sweater and making weeping sounds.

But it was just sounds. The tears hadn't come.

I had to admit, I was a pretty frozen-faced guy during my learning years as an actor. Keep in mind, I'd come in from six years in the army, most of it overseas. As a child I'd built up a hard core to deal with the difficulty at home; as an adult I'd layered on additional coats of armor to withstand the challenges hurled at me by soldiers below me and officers above me who chose, for a variety of reasons, to try to tee off on me. With all that resistance built up, I couldn't just toss it aside as one would dispose of a banana peel.

I remember talking with a lovely actress at the time, Marion Seldes. She was tall and very pretty, in a way that reminded me of my mother. We were strolling down 57th Street and could see a *New York Post* headline that said something along the lines of, "Massacre at Such-and-Such" or "Father Kills All His Children." I was discussing how inured I had become to elements of tragedy, which was something that I knew could be a flaw for an actor, but I felt unable to do anything about it. I pointed out the headline to Marion and said, "You see those headlines? They don't affect me at all. I'm cold to that sort of thing."

She said, "But, Jimmy, that's what we have to do. We have to learn to free ourselves, to be able to have full and free emotions."

As the chill November wind blew around us, I sighed, "Yeah, but I don't think I'll ever get it."

It's ironic, I suppose. When you get down to it, my entire acting ambition—which not only was I at a loss to grasp, but seemed to have sprung almost out of nowhere—was really an extension of everything that had happened in my life to that time. I'd spent my entire existence happening upon new ways of escaping—to other countries, to a war, to the air. Now Sandy Meisner's training was providing me with the ultimate escape—into another reality altogether. One where I could finally be totally, irrefutably in control.

No wonder I had such a drive to become skilled at it. If I'd become any more determined an escape artist, I could have rivaled Harry Houdini.

The summer of 1947 I spent at the Maverick Theater up near Woodstock, New York. It was composed of a company of actors from the senior class of the Neighborhood Playhouse. The Maverick was built as a little theater, had maybe 250 seats. It was good-sized, with a foyer. It was off in the woods. You had to know where the Maverick was; it wasn't the sort of place you'd casually drive past and say, "Oh, let's see what's playing here." Despite our low visibility, we drew in some pretty good audiences during our ten-week season. The shows even made a little money, although not for us. We never drew salaries, but we lived there and slept in little cabins, three or four people to each.

Lee Marvin joined the group. Lee had never been on stage before, never done anything. But he acted in a lot of our plays. Lee Marvin was, well, Lee Marvin, that's for sure. We'd be outside and suddenly he'd say, "Catch it, Jimmy!" I'd look up, and there would be a rifle coming straight at me. I'd have to reach up and catch it or it would hit me. He'd be checking my reaction to see how fast I was. I'd try the same stunt on him, but never even came close to catching him off guard or fazing him. He was a former marine, and he was *all* marine, that's for sure. He and I got along like a house afire. We had both done a lot of service during the war.

After our stint at the Maverick, we met one day on Seventh Avenue and 56th Street and stopped for coffee. He said, "My agent tells me I can get an awful lot more money if I go out to Hollywood . . . so I think I'll go out there."

"If you can do it, go ahead," I said. "I'm gonna miss you, though." I couldn't say I was surprised. He had done quite a few roles for us that summer. Not only was he good, but he was—I can't think of any other way to say it—a "Lee Marvin" type. A very specific type of guy that I had a feeling people would be asking for. I had a feeling he was going places.

Remember how I'd won a scholarship from the Academy of Radio Arts in Toronto, and it was on that that I had come to the Neighborhood Playhouse in New York? Well, when I returned to start my second year at the Playhouse, I met the latest winner of the scholarship. The newest Canadian arrival was a rubbery-faced young actor named Leslie Nielsen, and we became good buddies shortly thereafter.

Since I was in my second year, I helped him out as much as I could, as much as I knew how—which wasn't that much, I suppose. I liked him very much because he was one of these guys who never had any airs, never put any on. He was just a solid human being. He was also funny as hell, indulging in practical jokes (the cruder, the better) and then looking around in wide-eyed innocence when he was tagged as the culprit. The "wide-eyed innocence" all the funnier because he was so obviously behind whatever was going on. It wasn't until some years later that they finally invented the ideal Leslie Nielsen device—a fart machine, which he has carried with him for a quarter of a century now. He'll use it at inappropriate times (as if there's ever an appropriate time to uncork a serious fart) and then chastise the poor victim of his skewed humor. When he made his comedy breakthrough in *Airplane,* it may have surprised everyone who knew him as a deadly serious actor, but it shocked no one who had put up with his practical jokes back before it was stylish to laugh along with them.

Satisfying Sandy Meisner did not prove any easier than satisfying any other individual in my life. At one point we were mounting a production of *The Insect Comedy,* a play by Karel Capek, who also wrote *R.U.R.* This should be significant to science fiction fans, since Capek is credited with the first use of the word *robot* to mean mechanical man. R.U.R.

This is my very first picture—me with my mother, Sarah Frances Doohan, 1920.

My father, William Patrick Doohan. This was taken sometime after I returned home from the service.

Ever fascinated with things that go, here I am "driving."

Between two of my childhood chums— my sister, Margaret, and my pointer, Nell.

This is Kay Glynn. I had just finished my training.

My sister, Margaret, in one of my mother's creations.

Two cadets all turned out. That's Jim Stokes on the left.

My brother Bill with a bridesmaid outside the church where my brother Tom and his wife, Joan, were married.

I finally get to meet my grandmother. Here we are outside her house in Liverpool during the war, 1941.

Still in England, and still waiting to serve. This was taken in April 1943.

Here I am outside the theater of one of my earliest acting jobs, with my friend Johnny Carson.

One of my many parts in Canadian Broadcasting Company productions for television. Here, I play a psychiatrist trying to help emotionally disturbed girls.

The Neighborhood Playhouse School of the Theatre
16 WEST 46TH STREET.
NEW YORK 19. N. Y.

RITA WALLACH MORGENTHAU
                DIRECTOR

REBEKAH T. DALLAS
                REGISTRAR

DOROTHY K. MYERS
                SECRETARY

TELEPHONE
BRYANT 9-0766

July 15, 1946

Mr. James Doohan
c/o Mr. Lorne Greene
The Academy of Radio Arts
Toronto, Canada

Dear Mr. Doohan:

We are happy to accept you as a student of the
Neighborhood Playhouse School of the Theatre for the
season 1946-47. The opening day of school is October 1
at 9:30 A. M.

We offer our congratulations to you for we have
been informed by the Academy of Radio Arts that you have
been selected as "the most talented graduate", and will
be sponsored by them.

Attached you will find a list of books, which
should help provide you with background material for
lectures. It is advisable that you read these before
entrance.

A Medical Certificate is required on or before
October 1st.

We look forward to a pleasant relationship with
you during the coming season.

Sincerely,

Dorothy K. Myers

DOROTHY K. MYERS
Secretary

P. S.   Please fill out the enclosed application blank and
        return to me.
        On your first day of school, bring a pair of trunks
        and a "T" shirt so that you can participate in the
        Dance classes.

At the Maverick Theater in Woodstock, New York. This was a
very well received production of *Rope*.

Foreshadowing? A part in
Space Command, for the CBC.
This was touted as a "mature"
science fiction show for
younger viewers.

As always, a Ford man. Here I am working on the Mustang I owned during the shooting of *Star Trek*.

A publicity photo from the 1968–69 season of *Star Trek*.

From *Man in the Wilderness,* a role that I enjoyed immensely.

As a barrister in *The Trial of James McNeill Whistler.*

Star Trek: The Motion Picture had a marvelous engineering set.

Visitors to the set of *Star Trek: The Motion Picture.* Here I am with Wende and our son.

With Nick Meyers at the helm, the *Enterprise* crew returns in *Star Trek II: The Wrath of Khan.*

What I thought was Scotty's fitting tribute to a lost comrade.

Star Trek IV: The Voyage Home gave us all a chance to shine. Here I am with Walter Koenig.

Waiting between takes in San Francisco.

"Stan" and "Oliver" trying to work a computer.

Scotty returns in *Star Trek: The Next Generation.* Ron Moore's script was a moving tribute to everyone's favorite engineer.

On the bridge of the *Enterprise,* no "A, B, C, or D," with Patrick Stewart, who was great to work with.

At the Milwaukee School of Engineering, where I received an honorary degree—in engineering, what else.

The last appearance of Montgomery Scott, in *Star Trek Generations*.

stood for Rossum's Universal Robots. It comes from a Czech word meaning "forced labor or drudgery."

There was a kid who was cast in the role of a vagrant, and he wasn't "getting" it fast enough for Sandy. With five days to go before performance, Sandy said, "Jimmy, you're gonna have to take over this role. We start tomorrow morning at nine o'clock."

I said, "Fine." I went home, worked my butt off the entire night, and came in the next morning with the entire part memorized.

On my second day in the role, I was in the process of rehearsing a soliloquy about how abysmally we, as a species, tend to treat each other. It started, "Oh, God, I seem to see it all about me." I launched into the speech.

And Sandy, sitting in the last row, called out, "I don't believe you."

Gamely, I started again. "Oh, God, I seem to see it all about me . . ."

Again came an annoyed, "I don't believe you."

I was starting to get my Irish up. He'd flung me into this play at the last minute, presumably trusting that I could do the job, and he wasn't letting me get past the opening line.

"Oh, God, I seem to see it all about me . . ."

"I don't believe you."

Again and again, and finally, totally fed up, I jumped off the stage. I was ready to do *something* . . . storm out of the theater, or maybe storm right over Sandy, or something. From the look on his face, I got the feeling that Sandy felt I was ready to put my fist through it, and maybe he wasn't far wrong.

But he put a hand up and said consolingly, "Jimmy, Jimmy, just do what I *tell* you to do. C'mon now, you know . . ."

So I hauled myself back up onto the stage and, feeling very put upon, sighed, "Oh, God, I seem to see it all about me . . ."

Of course, *that* time it was believable.

In the summer of 1948, I didn't do any stage work. I went back to Toronto, along with Leslie Nielsen, visited my mom in the hospital, and did radio work to make a living. I did little summer shows and Department of Agriculture dramas on radio, including a twenty-minute soap opera called *The Craigs*. There was one time when I had to talk for twenty minutes straight on the gripping subject of erosion. That was tough—not to mention live—and I got an Ohio State award for it, which was the equivalent of the modern-day Emmy Award.

Then came 1949. . . .

11

The Year That Was

NINETEEN FORTY-NINE WAS A HELL OF A YEAR, BOTH ON A personal and a professional level. I experimented with some rather bizarre endeavors and encountered a few rather offbeat individuals—offbeat even when held against the yardstick of Leslie Nielsen, against whom all weirdness must be measured—and even became a song-and-dance man, although not all at the same time.

And the personal life, well, it wasn't exactly a stellar year for that.

I started the year sharing a cold-water flat with Johnny Fiedler on 65th Street off Broadway. A cold water flat means you get hot water, but there's no heat in the place. We had an electric heater that we had to turn off when we went to bed, lest we set the place on fire. On winter mornings it would be freezing. The bathtub was in the kitchen and the toilet was down the hall.

Johnny should be recognizable to *Star Trek* fans of all ages, from his appearance in the episode "Wolf in the Fold," where he played the secretly menacing Mr. Hengist. He is also the man behind the whispy-voiced portrayal of Piglet in the assorted Disney animated *Winnie-the-Pooh* shorts.

Actually, saying we shared the flat might be an exaggeration, because I'd be at the playhouse from nine A.M. to nine P.M., and Johnny would be out on the town from nine at night to nine in the morning. I'd get up and he'd be asleep.

It was around that time that Tony Randall (later famed for *The Odd Couple)* came up with the bright idea that we three—he, Johnny, and myself—should pursue singing careers.

I'd first met Tony when he had been coming around to Sandy's special classes. One day, as I said, Tony seized upon the notion that we should actively study singing. He said, "Let's go to Henry Jacobi." Jacobi was a voice-production teacher, who taught you how to produce the sound of your voice. Now, I had done a lot of singing, and I loved opera (as did Tony), and I was inclined to break out into song at any time.

Jacobi had a massive mouth full of teeth. He'd learned his techniques at the University of Madrid. He would relax you by giving you exercises called Poo-Tah, which were supposed to relax your vocal cords. Then he'd bring you up for your lesson.

I had a spare one hundred dollars, and Jacobi charged something like twenty dollars for twenty minutes, which was a chunk of change back then. So I told him, "I have one hundred dollars, so I'm here for five lessons." Tony did the same thing, and so did Johnny.

I swear to you, Jacobi had me with my mouth open, the note coming out and—like Ezio Pinza—I could not stop the note. I went into a conniption. I was doing C above high C—I had a range of about three and a half octaves—and I was holding a note with hardly any breath behind it.

Well, my second time there he said to me, "Jimmy, I will cut my price, and there's a lot of things you would have to do, but I swear to you I could have you in the Metropolitan in two years. But you will have to find the pianist and the person to teach you Italian and the music." Because Jacobi was strictly voice production. But I didn't pursue opera singing because of the money it would have required.

Ten years later I would mention this incident to Bill, and my brother said, "Oh, God, all you had to do was call me. The Veterans Administration would have paid for everything—the pianist, the singing lessons. All you had to do was have an expert like Jacobi say you were a singer!" The Canadian system was the second best in the world for veterans, with the Australian system the best. But I didn't know. Even now, to this day, I'll listen to some great tenor such as Pavarotti and a tear will come to my eye. What an opportunity I missed.

I spent the summer of 1949 at the Theater by the Sea in Matoonick, Rhode Island—ten weeks doing a different play every week. We'd be in production in one while rehearsing the next.

Our director was Billy Gilbert, a comedic actor whose ability to produce explosive sneezes was so formidable, that Walt Disney had immortalized him years earlier as the voice of Sneezy in *Snow White.* He was a very hands-on director; if you didn't do the line to his satisfaction, he'd give you a specific line reading to get it just right. Usually actors take a degree of umbrage at that, but it was impossible to become angry with Billy because he was just so brilliant. He had his wife with him, who was a Christian Scientist (as was he), and she was having a miserable summer because her father was dying of cancer.

Reta Shaw was another actress at the Theater by the Sea, a wonderful character actress who was in such films as *Mary Poppins* and was probably best known to TV fans for her regular role as the housekeeper in the series version of *The Ghost and Mrs. Muir,* with Hope Lange. Reta was terrific, a big girl with red hair and such a good actress; she knew what she was doing. She'd help you out if you didn't know what to do.

I also worked with a young guy named Jackie Gleason. Gleason was only two years away from his big break, with his appearances on *Cavalcade of Stars* in 1951 that would feature, among other characters, his landmark character of Ralph Kramden. But in 1949, he was toiling away in Rhode Island, hired by our theater to be in a show called *The Show Off,* not to mention as a comedian in an adjoining hotel.

If Jackie didn't like you, you had a tough time. I remember one incident, outside, between the hotel and the theater: Helmut Dantine, an Austrian actor, was in town doing the previous play with a Swedish actress named Signe Hasso. Gleason just hauled off and knocked Helmut down, and I have no idea why Jackie did it. It seemed to be just a case of Jackie saying, "I don't like you. *Wham!*" Poor old Helmut didn't know what to do.

There was a rather . . . interesting . . . actress playing the part of the mother in *The Show Off.* Her name was Nina Varella and she'd cut her acting teeth in the days of burlesque. She would travel the country as part of a variety act, and her best shtick involved her throwing out her arms and singing opera. She would hold a note for a minute or two, which required fabulous breath control. But it wasn't her command of her lungs, per se, that was her most prominent feature. No, after about twenty seconds of Nina's sustaining a note, her rather enormous breasts would begin to move, apparently of their own accord. First the right one, then the left, lifting up and going bump-bump-bump-bump. Then she could turn them in circles, left to the left, right to the right, and then she'd have them start ramming into each other.

She gave me and some of the guys a little show once. Talk about muscle control. Nonetheless, she was trying to carve a genuine acting career, feeling she had had enough of vaudeville.

Now, Jackie Gleason did not like Nina Varella, did not like her at all. Darned if I know how you can not like someone with dancing breasts. But he didn't take to her. She had the part, though, and she was good, and he knew she was good. He would throw extra lines at her, ad-libs, trying to trip her up. She stopped making eye contact with him, and he'd complain that she wasn't looking at him, making it difficult for him to act. When he wasn't around, she would say to me, "One of these days . . ." (although she didn't add to that, "Bang, zoom").

Jackie kept after her, every night, six nights a week, always trying to throw her off her acting stride. Well, the last night of the show, she had taken enough. She started answering him back, taking his ad-libs and topping them, and getting a lot of laughs. The audience, of course, didn't know that this wasn't part of the play.

In retaliation, Gleason started doing his night club act. For fifteen minutes, right there in the living room set, he brought the progress of the play to a halt as he did his stand-up. Nina sat there at the big, round dining room table, looking around and figuring, "What the hell . . . ?"

He would easily have gone on for another fifteen minutes or longer, but Nina walked up to him, tapped him on the shoulder, and said in a low and meaningful voice, "Do you want me to do *my* act now?"

That shut him up. He must have figured that dancing breasts would have gotten a standing ovation from the men in the audience while they were still in their seats.

By 1949, the nervous Canadian kid who was convinced that he would be thrown out of the New York Neighborhood Playhouse for lack of talent had become Sandy Meisner's assistant. It was at that point that I was approached by Nina Fonoroff, a Russian dance instructor. I'm sure she saw me as someone who was more or less game for anything—pretty much the way I had always been.

Nina had been working with another actor preparing a dance piece called *Mr. Puppet,* which was scheduled to be performed at the modern dance festival around the middle of

December. It was a public festival, and such acclaimed dancers as Martha Graham would be there, displaying their skills and routines.

Nina had decided that the actor she'd been working with wasn't "right." She came to me and said, "I would like you to do this. You speak during the piece, but I don't." It was rather a Pygmalion type of dance: I, the head puppet of the piece, would be trying to convince her that I think I'm alive. But I don't succeed, and in the end she dies, and her death kills me.

What do you expect from a Russian? Upbeat endings?

But, oh, that clever Doohan, always pushing the envelope and looking for new challenges, new frontiers. So every day, for six weeks I'd head down to her place in Greenwich Village, learning to be a puppet. I had to look like a puppet, with arms up and dangling like a marionette's. It was the hardest thing I had ever done in my life, and it wasn't made any easier by Nina's constant and impatient corrections. I wanted to shout, "I'm not a dancer! Go easy on me!"

When we did it at the modern dance festival, it was very well received. People were saying, "Oh, you're a dancer!" We also did this dance at the YMHA at 92nd Street, and at the Brooklyn Museum. Every time Nina wanted to do it, I would say, "Do we *have* to rehearse *that* again?" Finally we performed it at the Neighborhood Playhouse for Markova and Dolan, the famous modern dance team. They liked it so much that they bought the choreography from Nina and took her with them for the whole summer to Europe.

It was a job, certainly a fun thing to do, but one of the hardest jobs of my life. It was nothing I wanted to pursue on a regular basis, even though, for some reason, women found a dancer to be very much a turn on. But for me dancing wasn't worth the effort, and besides, turning on assorted women wasn't a major priority—because I also got married in 1949.

What a disaster that was. The end result was four terrific children, but the marriage itself . . . well, I really should have had an annulment after ten days. If I had been able to talk to anybody about it, I likely would have, but my brothers were miles away and it was just impossible. So I never really considered it as a possibility.

Mainly, it was a mistake because of my being Catholic and Janet not. Even though she promised to live up to my Catholic standards, she didn't really mean it.

It's ironic, really. She wanted to marry me for a reason that, at its core, I could really understand: she wanted to get away from a parent she couldn't stand. In this case, it was her mother. Her mother came to visit us in New York, and it was sort of like, "Well, what are you two going to do? Are you going to get married?"

And I thought, *"Ooohhh* shit." I really didn't want to do it. But the loss of Kay still stung me, and I had said to myself, "God, the next woman that loves me, I will marry." I thought she loved me. It turned out she didn't.

We came back from the honeymoon, and a married girlfriend of Janet's came to visit. The girlfriend was pregnant, and upon seeing her Janet thought, *Oh, God, that's going to happen to me, because he's Catholic. He's not using condoms or anything else.*

And damned if she didn't bring her mother and father into the bedroom to talk about the subject to me. They said, "Why don't you use these things?"

To say I was uncomfortable discussing it is to understate the matter. Janet had said she understood, she'd promised she'd understood, and now I was being asked—ordered—to justify very personal beliefs. "Because it's against my religion," I said. That's when I should have been smart enough to choose an annulment. I'm sure the church would have supported me.

But instead I stuck it out for seventeen years. You can't always be looking for a way to escape from an undesirable situation. So instead of trying to escape, I chose to stay and fight for something I believed in: a Catholic marriage.

Frankly, Normandy was a hell of a lot easier.

12

Jimmy Hollywood

MY CAREER WAS BLOSSOMING IN THE 1950S EVEN AS MY PERSONAL life was becoming a shambles. My marriage was hardly becoming any more loving, but that was almost the least of it. I lost both my mother and my father to illness. That was hard enough, even though neither death came as a complete shock to me. My mother had been hospitalized for nine years, and as for my father, well, after all the years of drinking . . . But the worst was the death of my poor sister, Margaret, in 1955. As I mentioned, she'd never been a particularly strong or healthy woman. But her body finally gave out, after an emergency operation failed to save her. I was there with her, holding her, and I heard her last breath rattling in her throat. She was thirty-seven years old. She had never married, never had children, never really had a fair chance at a life. I had never cried as hard as I did at that moment.

If I could have earned a living on the stage, I would have. I still feel that way. I love the instant reaction from the crowd. No matter what, you have to try to do the same thing every night, but it's not really the same thing. If somebody watches one night and then comes back the next night, they think they're seeing exactly the same thing each time, but they're not.

But there were other opportunities becoming available—radio, and the thriving realm of television. In 1950, I told Sandy Meisner that I didn't want to be his assistant anymore, that I wanted to build my own acting career. But at the same time, I had some hesitation. We were walking around the block and I said, "What do you think my chances are?"

He said, "Jimmy, you have been a hard worker, and you have lots of talent. Just keep on going, and what will happen to you in the future depends on the number of roles you get and the directors you get. If you ever get into trouble, just go back and think of what I taught you. But I tell you, no matter what, it'll still take you twenty years to be an actor. Because it'll take you twenty years to think through everything, to lose yourself. You've got to think—not of yourself—you've got to think of how to do it. It's your body and the technical parts of your body that are producing this character. Once you start thinking of yourself, you will not be successful. You will not do the character properly."

And he would turn out to be right. It would take me two decades before I would finally say to myself, "Okay, now I don't give a damn what they throw at me. I can do it."

My first television work was in a show called *Martin Kane, Private Eye,* and I played a detective. William Gargan was the star; he was an old B-movie star. A really sweet man, and I guess he was hoping to make a comeback.

I did fifty-five live broadcasts in New York. Then I went to Toronto, walked into the Canadian Broadcasting offices, which had just started up three weeks before, and walked out with six months work.

My bookings piled up, one atop another, as I ping-ponged between Canada and New York. Next thing I knew, I had a year and a half's work lined up. My fellow Canadian actors, knowing that I had come up from New York, assumed I was American and said resentfully, "This Yankee's got in here;

this American . . ." and I told them, "Hey, I was here before. I'm from Sarnia, Ontario."

When one thinks of acting and the 1950s, invariably one thinks about "the blacklist" and the House Un-American Activities Committee, with their relentless and frightening search for Communists in every corner and under every bedsheet. I had my own problems with the HUAC around 1951. I had gotten on a show called *Treasury Men in Action,* which also occasionally featured my Maverick Theater compatriot, Lee Marvin. It was directed by David Pressman, who was also a teacher at the Neighborhood Playhouse, had been taught by Sandy way back, and, as it so happens, really *was* a Communist.

David was directing the show, and I was being hired about every two weeks as one of the Treasury Secret Service guys. It was a semiregular job, and I'd show up twice a month to see if there was a part for me. David usually found something for me, and I certainly never dwelt on whether he was a Communist. It certainly didn't bother me at the time.

So one time I went to the agency that ran the show and I said, "Could I see David Pressman, please?"

"Oh, he's not here anymore," the receptionist said. Looking mildly suspicious, she said, "Who are you?"

"I've been on some of your shows, maybe every second week . . ."

"Why don't you go down to see Miss So-and-So?" she said. I went down, figuring that she was a casting agent or something.

It quickly became clear that, whatever she was an agent for, it wasn't casting. Miss So-and-So asked me question after question along the lines of, "Did you know David? Did you know anything about him?"

Confused, I told her of what little interaction I'd had with David at the Neighborhood Playhouse. I had no idea what this woman wanted from me. I found out later that somebody had turned David in as a Communist. It was mentioned in what was called *Red Channels* (a directory of entertainers and announcers who were alleged to be suspect).

It was a horrible thing. Somebody could just call you a Communist and you didn't work, even if it wasn't true. Another actor, (who's quite well known today) and I were up for the lead in a series. After a lengthy audition process it came down to just him and me. He got the part, and I never even got onto any of the shows.

About seven months later, an agent I used to check with named Jules Ziegler said, "Remember that series thing? It's very strange, but I found out that actor told everybody you were a Communist and that's why he got the part."

I tell you, I've never liked him since. That's the kind of slimy, really awful stuff that some people do just to get ahead.

People really went crazy about Communism. I always figured we could beat the Russians no matter what, because we know how to do things. It never bothered me one little bit; I figured any time somebody wanted to fight, we would handle it and we would win, so they'd better not mess with us. That's the way I thought it would turn out, and that's how it turned out.

Between my work in both New York and Canada, I never gave any thought to Hollywood at all. It was three thousand miles away, and that was too much for me—too much of a relocation, too far away from everything I knew. Besides, Who needed movies? as far as I was concerned. Over the next eight years, from 1950 to 1958, I think I did 450 live television shows. I did one damn near every week for eight years. I did four thousand radio shows also during that time. After only a year, I was being called Canada's Busiest Actor.

I found there was very little I had to do to make the transition between stage, radio, and television. I just didn't make things quite as "big" on television. I quickly found that if a director knows you've done a lot of stage, he'll tell you, "Back off here, don't talk so loudly, you don't have to be so specific in what you're saying." On stage, your voice has to be able to carry. (That's less so nowadays, though, what with the tiny hidden microphones stage actors can carry with them.)

I can't say the audition process was always demanding. On one show called *Suspense,* I was sent up to read for the producer and director, Robert Stephens. I knocked at the door, went in, and he handed me a piece of paper. "Read," was all he said.

I proceeded to read for the part of a Bengal Lancer officer. I got through two lines, and Stephens barked, "You're hired. Out."

I guess it was better than, "Don't quit your day job. Out."

In those days, many writers had zero idea how to time out a script. We'd get sixty-, seventy-, ninety-page scripts for a half-hour show. Characterization was lost, scenes had no point. Oftentimes it would be up to the actors, sitting around a table, to cut up the script. We'd cut lines: "I don't need to say this." "Yeah, but he needs this here." We'd whack it down to a manageable length.

Of course, this process wasn't required for writers such as Paddy Chayefsky. At least never on anything I worked on. Either Paddy was high quality going in, or he learned exceptionally quickly before I ever came on the scene.

On my fifth segment of *Suspense,* around ten in the morning we were blocking the show and I got severe pain in my gut. It got worse and worse, and Robert Stephens was barking, "What's the matter with you!"

I just said, "I'm sorry," and tried not to groan.

During lunch I shot back to where we were living at the time and consulted with a little old Jewish doctor who was living downstairs. He poked around and said, "You better get to the hospital right away, because that's your appendix."

I said, "I've got a show, and it won't be over until nine o'clock." I figured that all I had to do to ruin my career was to miss a show.

I did the episode, working through the rapidly escalating pain. The moment the show was finished, I staggered out to a cab, which sped me to New York Hospital. The little old

Jewish doctor had set it all up. I went in and was operated on within twenty minutes. By the next morning, they had me on my feet.

I went back to see Stephens, and he said, "I don't want to see you anymore! That was a terrible show you did!"

"But . . . but I had to have an emergency appendectomy!" I sputtered.

"I don't care!" he snapped. And I never worked for him again.

A pity, really. If only the part I'd been playing had called for me to be in agony for the entire segment, Stephens might have made me a regular.

By the late 1950s, all the people that I had used to know in New York had all moved to Hollywood. Leslie Nielsen was already there; Eli Wallach, after 1957; it seemed everyone was off to Hollywood. Having reached a point in my career where I felt there were no more horizons for me to reach where I was, I knew it was time to move forward.

Living in Toronto at the time, I bought a TR-3, a Triumph with two seats—black with a white convertible top—and drove out to Hollywood. I stayed with Leslie and went to see some agents he introduced me to, armed with kinescopes of things I'd done. There seemed to be genuine interest, genuine possibilities. We, the family and I, made the jump out to Hollywood.

I was called away from Hollywood to do an eight-episode serialization of a novel called *Wings of Night,* based on life in Nova Scotia. I played a woodsman. That was a fun part to do.

There was one sequence where I was in a canoe with my "guide," paddling down a river. The script called for us to go over a waterfall that was about fifteen feet wide, and the drop was about six feet. The character of the guide was supposed to be an American Indian, but the actor was really British and knew absolutely nothing about canoeing. I at least had *some* experience, thanks to the time I'd spent at Lake Aquila in Cleveland with my cousins, the Schneiders.

So I told the "guide," "All you have to do is sit straight. We're going down with the left side of the canoe first, but we're going to lean a bit to the right and just slide down. The only way we can really go down properly in a canoe is sideways. It'll be a piece of cake; just do what I tell you." He did, and we did it in one shot. I would have loved to do that part again.

After that I went to Montreal to rehearse a French-Canadian melodrama for the author-producer-star Gratien Gelina. I hated the part, probably more than any other I've ever played in my life, because the character was just so one-note evil. He had a soul and personality black as pitch, no saving grace to him at all. We were to do it at the 1962 Seattle World's Fair. Getting to the World's Fair was my only reason for doing the part.

Back in Hollywood, I did an episode of *Bewitched.* I did two episodes of *Bonanza*—one of them with Majel Barrett, although we didn't have any scenes together. I did an episode of *The Rogues,* which featured David Niven, Gig Young, and Charles Boyer.

One of the marks of courtesy that actors extend to each other is being there to deliver lines from off-camera. Keep in mind that whenever you see any sort of angle where someone isn't in the shot, *technically* they aren't really needed there when it's filmed. However, if they *are* delivering their lines from off-camera, it aids the performance of the actor on camera. It's a matter of courtesy and caring about the other actors' giving the best performance possible.

Just to contrast: On *Bonanza,* when it was time for your close-up, the script girl would read the lines of whomever you were talking to. Lorne and the others were back in their dressing rooms talking business with someone or other.

Now, David Niven on *The Rogues* was the exact opposite. He would be there, off-camera, delivering the lines, being helpful and supportive of his fellow actors. Of course, it's only natural that he expected a similar courtesy in return. I'll never forget one occasion when it was David's close-up, and the scene involved his speaking with someone who had a glass of champagne in his hand. And the other fellow who was in the scene came up with a paper cup instead of a glass.

And David said in that polished accent of his, "Please don't bring a paper cup on when you had a glass in your hand before. Why did you even make me think about that? I have other things to think about. Please, always do everything properly, the way you did it when you were doing the scene and when you did your close-up." Boy, was the guy embarrassed, and it was a good lesson for me.

(And yes, in case you're wondering, on *Star Trek* we would always be there for one another to read dialogue from off-camera.)

The very first movie I did in Hollywood was *The Wheeler Dealers,* which starred James Garner, Lee Remick, and Jim Backus. Arthur Hiller was directing it. I'd worked for Arthur before back in Canada, on the first half-hour TV show he'd ever directed, as a matter of fact, after he'd taken the Canadian Broadcasting Corporation's directing course.

I had a nice little chat with James Garner before we started shooting. The scene was in a courtroom, and I was his lawyer. He was on the right, and I was on the left. Hiller came up and said, "We'll start in the middle and then go around to the left. It'll take us about ten days to shoot this whole courtroom scene."

But Jim Garner said to him, "No, why don't you start on the other side of him, so my scenes with my lawyer will come later?" Hiller shrugged and went along with it, because it was all the same to him. But Garner said to me afterward, "That angle puts you in more shots. That gives you ten more days work!" He's that kind of a guy. Still is, as far as I'm concerned. The only people who ever say anything nasty about him are the studios who are trying to rip him off.

By 1964, I was still working briskly enough, but my marriage was in its death throes. Our union had produced four children: two boys, Montgomery John and Christopher, who are fraternal twins, and two girls, Larkin and Deirdre. For nearly seventeen years it had been a loveless marriage, and in that sort of situation, one never knows what the final straw will be. As it turned out, it happened one morning in our Los Angeles home. I was up at seven o'clock, getting the kids up and off to school. She was still in bed, as she always was. I was hustling the kids around, "Get up, kids, get dressed."

She finally sauntered down about eight-thirty, just before they got off to school. She stood there with a critical eye and said, "What the hell kind of clothes did you put on them?"

I just blew up. She had done nothing around the house, nor did she ever. I was the one who got them up, got them breakfast, did everything for them. I did the laundry for the kids when the clothes were dirty. She wouldn't do it.

And so I said to myself, "That's it. I can't stay any longer."

Leaving the kids was hard . . . very hard. The marriage had been sour, but they were as sweet as can be. The two girls are beautiful. Larkin, has four children of her own (although her own marriage ended in divorce) and now lives in Tacoma. Deirdre wound up marrying a sergeant (now a lieutenant) in the Oakland police—a really nice guy named Louis Cruz. Deirdre has two children.

Montgomery John is the eldest of the twins—highest IQ in the family, with a great work ethic. When he does a job, that job is done right: a good carpenter, a good plumber, and a good engineer (of course). He's one of the greatest fishermen in Los Angeles. He wins prizes all the time. He has a Ford Ranger with a camper on top, as well as a fishing boat, and he's having a hell of a good time with that.

As for Christopher, he's also a very sharp boy. He started operating CAT scans in hospitals and became as correct in his diagnosis of various ailments as the doctors were. He's had a band for the last ten years or so. They were doing rock and roll and drowning out his singing voice, and at my suggestion they recorded an album with country songs. He sent me a fax the other day saying Columbia Records was interested. He has two children, two little girls.

But as well as the kids turned out, at the time I was in dire straits.

Fortunately enough, my old friend Leslie Nielsen stepped in. There had been a time when Leslie had been dirt poor, starving, and I'd helped him out. I kept giving him money until he finally told me he didn't need help.

So now it was some years later, my marriage had broken up, and I was living in Mae West's hotel, just south of Melrose. He called up the house and found out where I was staying. Next thing I knew, Leslie was on the phone, saying, "Pack up your stuff and get up here. You're a guy who doesn't like to live alone, so you come up and live with us."

I was worried about imposing and wanted to make sure it was okay with Leslie's wife, Sandy. With my own marriage shattered, the last thing I wanted to do was risk putting a strain on someone else's. But Sandy made it clear that it was all right with her. So I moved into his house way up in the Hollywood Hills, and later they took me along to their new home in Beverly Hills, a big Spanish colonial house.

At that point neither of us was working that much, so we had a ball redecorating the house. One day I was doing something in the dining room, and all of a sudden I heard a *smash.*

I shouted, "God, what are you *doing?!*"

"I'm working," Leslie called back in that calm, measured tone he always affected that served to cover his somewhat skewed activities.

So I thought, *Oh, okay . . . he's working.* And then there was another *smash,* even louder than the first. He was tearing something down in the kitchen that he didn't like. I ran in there to discover that the place looked—and I had valid basis for comparison—like London during the Blitz.

He did wind up bringing in a carpenter, though, which nicely averted his destroying the whole house. The man was a

Scotsman, as a matter of fact. The kitchen wound up being beautiful, and then we started on other parts of the house. The house had bathrooms that had the most fantastic tile work, and there was a section of the house off the kitchen, which was where I lived.

I just had an awfully good time with them. I remember Bob Goulet coming to see Leslie and sitting around drinking. At the time, neither Bob nor I was working, although Leslie was getting a fair amount of work.

What's ironic is that he was busy building a career on straitlaced roles and, years later, he would build a new career parodying the exact types of roles for which he'd first become noted. But anyone who knew Leslie for the comedian and practical joker that he was wasn't the least bit surprised. He'd come up with the most outrageous situations, the most absurd statements, and then look at you with this utterly proper deadpan and say, "I wouldn't lie to you . . . so you know it's the truth."

Then, shortly thereafter, although Bob still wasn't working, I got a job in a television series.

Depending upon how you look at it, it lasted three seasons . . . or three decades. I know that sounds absurd, but I wouldn't lie to you, so you know it's the truth.

13

Show-time

KEEP IN MIND THAT I ALMOST WOUND UP NOT HAVING A "TYPICAL day" on the set of *Star Trek*.

When we shot the pilot in 1965, it took them quite a while to get word to us of whether we were a go or not. Word didn't come down from Desilu that the pilot had sold until the beginning of 1966. And I thought, *Oh, great, I have a running job here.* My contract was for nine out of thirteen shows.

Three or four days after hearing that the pilot had sold, I got a letter from Gene Roddenberry saying, "Thanks very much, but we don't really think we're going to need an engineer." I think they were probably trying to save money. I got the letter about eleven o'clock in the morning, and I called my agent, Paul Wilkins. Paul was pissed because the letter should have gone to the agent. He said, "You just wait there. We'll see about this." I could tell from the tone of his voice and the pauses he took that he was trying to hold his temper.

He went to Gene Roddenberry and Herb Solow, Herb being the executive in charge of production on behalf of Desilu. Paul was not one who was easily ignored. He was six foot two, slim, with silvery dark hair. Then Paul called me and said, "You're back on the show." I didn't have a commitment for "every show produced"; they only signed me on for some of the episodes.

Nonetheless, over the three seasons they discovered the usefulness of the engineer and the engineering room—a room that expanded from one season to the next. (Compare the one-room environment of the first season to the multileveled, vastly expanded engineering area by the third.) One of the axioms of television drama is "show, not tell." If the *Enterprise* engines were in dire straits or the dilithium crystals drained, it was far better to cut to Scotty pacing his engine room while delivering the bad news, than just to let the captain know over the intercom.

The show was quite fabulous in those days, and it was all brand-new. Not that there was much in the way of support from Paramount. Paramount really did not understand or know what to do with *Star Trek.* They had purchased Desilu, which was of interest to them for its production facilities and such shows as *Mission: Impossible.* That series was more fun for them, more accessible. They could understand that show.

My average "set call" (the time that I had to be on the set by) for *Star Trek* was usually seven o'clock in the morning. I'd drive there on my own, in my black Mustang fastback, rather than have a studio driver pick me up. The average drive time was twenty minutes to the studio entrance at 5555 Melrose Avenue. I'd pull onto the lot to a designated parking area. I didn't have a parking space with my name painted on it, although Bill Shatner and Leonard Nimoy did.

We did, however, all have our own designated dressing rooms— although we were shoved in together for the filming of the pilot. (I roomed with George Takei. It was a hell of a way to meet a future friend and coworker, two people being crammed into a room barely large enough for one.) When I'd arrive, I'd check that the costume was there, and then head to makeup.

It was cold in the makeup room, although not quite cold

enough to make your breath mist up. Of course, you liked that on days when temperatures were going to be one hundred degrees. Under ordinary circumstances, I'd be in and out in about ten minutes or less. Leonard was already gone by the time I arrived, with a set call of at least six o'clock to deal with his Spock makeup. Women, with their elaborate hairdos, would be called in even earlier, five-thirty.

Breakfast would be prepared for us. The "crafts services" people, who were in charge of catering, would ask what we wanted. When I was a kid, I'd been a big breakfast guy, chowing down on a big bowl of cornflakes, four eggs scrambled, four slices of toast. But by the time I was in my mid forties and on the set of *Star Trek,* I was perfectly happy with a ham-and-egg sandwich on toast, just about every day. Eventually I just said, "The usual."

We would sit around in our dressing rooms, waiting to be called down to the set. Nichelle and I used to do the *Los Angeles Times* crossword puzzle. By the end of the third season I could shoot right through them because of the constant repetition of clues. By about the twentieth time that you've come up with the original name of Tokyo (Edo), it gets a bit dull.

If I got bored with that, I'd borrow a copy of one of the trade publications, like *Variety,* from someone.

So much of television and movies simply involves waiting around. Fortunately, I was an old hand at biding my time. After all, I had sat around for five years waiting for my first major foray into World War II so I could step in front of a bullet. So waiting around for a few hours to step in front of a camera was a good deal easier.

Usually I'd be down on the set by eight in the morning. The *Star Trek* set was a pretty loose one. People would be sitting around, chatting. George was a pretty good talker, chatting it up with De (DeForest Kelley) or Leonard. Bill was always off in his dressing room, generally keeping to himself.

To visitors or outsiders, the idea of making a television show seems like the most exciting thing in the world. But, I tell you, day in, day out, it could be remarkably tedious. When you're not sitting around waiting, then you're in front of the camera and having to do the same dialogue over and over again, first for the master shot, then for your close-up or for an over-the-shoulder shot where you're addressing someone else.

Since everything is so much on the fly, there's not a lot of time to get your lines down. Generally, I was off book, my lines memorized, fairly quickly. It was an old habit I'd gotten down from my days on live television. I can remember there were a lot of shots that they wouldn't take of me until the end of the day, when everybody else had gone home, because they knew I would zip right through them. That would sometimes be four or five little lines; they'd relight quickly and take each shot.

The best directors were Marc Daniels and Joe Pevney. They did the whole second year, switching off every other week. That's a murderous pace to maintain, because either you are in the middle of shooting an episode, or you're in the middle of "prepping" for the next week's show. It's like directing on a treadmill.

Generally, you don't bother to think about what they've asked you to do. You just do it. If there's anything to argue about, you argue about it. Sometimes directors would say, "I want you to do so-and-so," and I would reply, "That's not the way to do it. That's not the way *we* would do it." They'd have to defer to us because we were the regulars.

On some television programs, particularly half-hour formats, "table readings" are held. That involves the entire cast sitting around a table doing a reading of the script, just to get a feel for the basic dynamics. But we didn't do that on *Star Trek*. There wouldn't be a read-through when we got a new script. We'd finish one script by noon and come back in the afternoon to start the next one. They'd say, "We're gonna start with scene forty after dinner."

It's not a process that's particularly supportive of character development or giving thought to what's happening in the story.

Still, all things considered . . . we had an exciting little series, of which I was in half. Not all the episodes were memorable, and some of them I'd just as soon forget.

Here are some of the highlights (and lowlights):

"The Corbomite Maneuver": (The *Enterprise* is paralyzed by a huge vessel and informed that she'll be blown up in a few minutes.)

The main thing I remember was how utterly bizarre our little alien looked in that episode. He was played by Clint Howard (brother of now-director Ron Howard), and I had never seen anyone quite as strange-looking as he. He was absolutely marvelous, and he was so cute. He seemed to take it all in stride, walking around with that makeup.

"Mudd's Women": (Con artist Harry Mudd boards the ship with a trio of gorgeous women who may not be what they seem.)

Unsurprisingly, this is one you remember by thinking of the girls. I remember in particular Susan Denberg, a German girl who played Magda and also appeared as a centerfold playmate of the month. When they were shooting the sequences where we're supposed to be ogling the women, I didn't consider that an acting challenge. I looked on her and sort of thought, *Wooooeeee.* She was just a super-looking girl, but I never bothered to approach her. There are some girls I look at and I say to myself, "Well, they're probably taken anyway."

"The Enemy Within": (Kirk is split into good and evil versions of himself.)

A remarkably daring episode when you think about it. How many series, in one of their first half-dozen episodes, have an entire plotline involving the heroic lead's darkest rape fantasies? Whenever I see photos from that, I know which episode it is, because the "evil" Kirk's eyebrows are a little weirder. I thought Bill's performance was pretty okay in that one.

The Naked Time": (A bizarre virus causes everyone to lose their inhibitions.)

Most people remember that one for George running around with his fencing foil. I'll certainly always remember that, since I was the one who nearly got a sword through his skull when George was practicing with the thing. In his own defense, George has talked about how he was off practicing in a secluded area of the soundstage and I "interrupted" his practice. George is my dear friend, and that's why I say two words here to George: "dressing room." Wave it around in seclusion, George.

He's lucky it was just me that he scared witless. If it had been one of the teamsters, they'd probably have made him eat the sword.

Kevin Riley's singing "I'll Take you Home Again, Kathleen" brought back fond memories. It was one of my favorite songs when I was growing up. My mother taught it to me.

This was the episode with one of Scotty's oft-quoted lines. Upon learning that the engines have been shut down and that it will take longer to restart them than they have before their orbit decays, an anguished Scotty says, "I canna change the laws of physics!"

This was coming from an engineer aboard a ship that defies Einstein with its faster-than-light travel and has a matter transporter that flies in the face of the Heisenberg Uncertainty Principle. Okay, okay, maybe Scotty couldn't change the laws of physics. But he sure could bend them a good ways.

"The Galileo Seven": (A shuttlecraft with Spock, McCoy, Scotty, a yeoman, and several red-shirted security men who have "target" painted on their back are stranded on a hostile world while the *Enterprise* searches for them in futility.)

Oftentimes the crew had to depend upon Scotty's engineering expertise, but it was rare that people had to risk tripping over him while he was exercising it. I spent much of the episode on my belly with my face in the floorboard engineering systems of the cramped shuttle. The most memorable aspect of the episode for me was that it was the first opportunity I had to work closely with Leonard. We'd had scenes before, but it was the first time we worked just one-on-one. Leonard was easy to like from the get-go, as sincere, thorough, and professional an actor as one could hope to work with.

"The Squire of Gothos": (The crew finds itself the plaything of a childish alien entity called Trelane.)

It was the first time that I was in an episode as someone other than Scotty. To be specific, I was the voice of Trelane's father. I did that in a couple of other episodes as well. I was the voice of Sargon in "Return to Tomorrow" and the Melkotian in "Spectre of the Gun."

I told the producers that I could do a lot of other characters, and I tried to impress on them that if they wanted a voice, they should let me know. I could do a lot. I gave them examples. It was nice to receive another fee for the voice-overs. I was always looking for a running part like that, similar to what Majel Barrett had with the computer voice.

I got to know Bill Campbell, who played Trelane, and we became very good friends. Bill and I would see each other and play Liverpool rummy; I'd go out to see him at his house and talk. I met his brother, who's a writer and very good, too.

Bill's wife, Theresa, is something else. She is Yugoslavian, and Bill had met her while doing a movie over there. She was in charge of the script, like a script girl. She could speak four or five different languages, Italian, Yugoslavian, German, English. She loved Bill, he loved her, and they're still together, doing just fine.

He's a talker, there's no doubt about that. And an awful lot of it is bullshit—but it's interesting if you want to sit down and listen. He knows an awful lot of people. He knew all sorts of old actors, and he was instrumental in getting me out to the Motion Picture Home to do some charity work. For about a year and a half, every Thursday, I would go into town and get the *TV Guide*s that the publisher donated to the home. I'd pick them up at an office, and I'd deliver them to the home, one to each room or house, and leave a batch of thirty or forty in the wards, where the nurses could use them for the bedridden or incapacitated.

"Arena": (Kirk fights a lizardlike alien called a Gorn on a desert world.)

This is one of those instances where memory plays tricks on you. When people asked me what I didn't like about science fiction, I always complained about all these aliens who happen to speak English. And I would hold up "Arena" as an example of that. I would say, "Even Lizard monsters speak English!"

Except in reviewing some of the episodes in preparation for this work, I discovered that exactly the opposite is true for "Arena." It is, in fact, the one episode where we see a translator device being used, as the Gorn's snarling and growling is interpreted for Kirk's edification.

What's impressive is that I've been mistakenly talking about the Gorn being able to speak perfect English for years now . . . and *no one* has ever corrected me on it. Which means that either everyone in *Star Trek* fandom has as faulty a memory as I or, the more likely, the fans were just too polite to say anything.

"A Taste of Armageddon": (The *Enterprise* gets caught between two worlds that wage war by computer.)

Poor Gene Lyons, who played Ambassador Fox, was simply out of his element. He was completely discombobulated for some reason. It took him many takes to get it, and they finally went to having him speak off-screen. He had a really good look to him, but just couldn't get the lines down.

It's likely that he was just thrown off by the unusual nature of the show. I think he started out okay and then got really confused because of the amount he had to say. I really feel sorry for a guy in that state.

"Tomorrow Is Yesterday": (Not to be confused with "Return to Tomorrow" or "All Our Yesterdays," this was our first major time-travel story if one doesn't count the brief time-reversal jaunt in "The Naked Time." The *Enterprise* is hurled into the 1960s and has to take extreme caution not to change the time line.)

It was the first time that I did one of my "miracle moves." The ship was in an unprecedentedly difficult situation, and Scotty (with Spock) came up with a plan to get us out of it. The special effects (shaking the ship slightly, that sort of thing) seem primitive compared to what you see nowadays. But back then we were cutting edge and the viewership was willing to take a good deal on faith. As opposed to today's far more literal-minded fans, who scrutinize every effect and hold it up to the highest standards.

During one sequence when the *Enterprise* is straining to get back to her own time, I'm shown being thrown against the background grid and clutching on to it for all I'm worth. It was such a dynamic-looking shot that they wound up using it in other episodes, such as "The Doomsday Machine."

"Space Seed": (The *Enterprise* comes across a sleeper ship containing eighty "Napoleons" from old Earth, including their leader, Khan—played by Ricardo Montalban.)

This was the basis for *Star Trek II: The Wrath of Khan.* That was a superior *Star Trek* movie, although "Space Seed" wasn't our best episode. There was the troubling story point that a Starfleet officer, Marla McGivers (Madlyn Rhue), was quickly swept into a relationship with Khan that was abusive, even borderline sadistic on Khan's part. He tossed her around; he badgered her, he generally treated her like garbage. It was bad enough that he handled her that way, but she took to it so quickly that she committed an act of treason against her crew mates.

Plus the fight scene in engineering, while was nicely choreographed, made extensive and unfortunately *very* obvious use of Bill's stunt double, Gary Coombs. Stuntmen are most effective in quick cuts, but Coombs was on screen for relatively lengthy sequences, with Bill only in tight close-ups.

And, I'm sorry, but I think Scotty, being a good Scotsman, *would* have been up on his Milton.

What held the episode together, however, was Ricardo, a larger-than-life style of actor. I think it was a great pity he wasn't nominated for an Oscar for *The Wrath of Khan.* Very few people ever did as good a job on screen as he did in *Wrath.*

I actually didn't get to work with him much in either of his *Trek* appearances. But I worked with him on *Fantasy Island.* I played a French fop from three hundred years ago. Credit Aaron Spelling, who never bought into the entire typecasting game and had no problem hiring me.

"The Menagerie": (A two-parter incorporating the unsold *Star Trek* pilot "The Cage"; Spock defies regulations to bring his former commander to a forbidden world.)

Susan Oliver, a lovely young actress who died far, far too young—in her late forties, I believe—guest-starred in that episode. Susan was one of my students at the Neighborhood Playhouse. "Susan Oliver" was her stage name, her real name having a very German or Dutch sound to it.

I can remember standing in front of Cromwell's drugstore, talking to Susan about the business. Cromwell's drugstore was a sort of gathering place for actors, in the RCA Building on Sixth Avenue. It was a darn good restaurant, with the best BLT on wheat you ever had. Tony Randall, Anne Jackson, Eli Wallach would hang out there.

It was a great way to connect for jobs. Actors would tell you, "You'd be right for such-and-such a part; go around and see them." Everybody was everybody else's agent back then; no agents would accept you unless you were a big star in New York. In Hollywood you had to have an agent before you could go anywhere. You didn't have an "in" at all, you couldn't call up a producer and say, "Could I come around and see you?"

Susan said to me, with tears in her eyes, "Oh, Jimmy, I just don't think I'm ever going to get any work." I comforted her and assured her that things would turn around for her. It was tough enough to get work; I had done some more than she had, but nobody was hiring Susan Oliver.

But within a year or two, I was up in Toronto working and, sure enough, I was seeing Susan on the screen all the time.

Years later, Susan and I were at a *Star Trek* convention, and we were up in my room talking. I never made a move on her; I used to be her teacher, after all, and so it felt like a sort of honor thing. We just talked until four o'clock in the morning, discussing the infinite variations on the simple premise that nothing could beat love.

And she had her own plane. She loved to fly; if she had a show in San Francisco, she flew up there in her own plane.

"The Devil in the Dark": (Miners are menaced by a rocklike creature called a Horta, which turns out to be a mother protecting its young.)

What a lovely show. I just thought it was one of the best. It had such a seat-of-the-pants origin, with master monster-actor Janos Prohaska crawling into Gene Coon's office in the Horta costume. "What is that?!" asked Gene.

"I don't know," said Janos. "I just made it."

"Well, I'm going to write an episode around it," said Gene. And he did, and it was true science fiction. I loved the script when I read it, thought it was great. It might also be one of the best uses of the mind-meld I've ever seen, with Spock linking directly to the creature to read its mind.

Of course, the setup and ending do leave one scratching one's head ever so slightly. A Horta consuming rocks isn't the same as a herbivorous animal eating plants, because the plants grow back. The rocks won't. Sooner or later, the Hortas are literally going to eat themselves out of house and home. Oh, sure, they die en masse every fifty thousand years, but when you give it some thought, you realize that the Hortas are a race with a limited term of existence, destroying their planet as they go and gearing toward eventual extinction.

Hmm. Not completely unlike humans, when you stop to think of it.

For those who collect bits of trivia: It's the only episode with a teaser that features none of the *Enterprise* crew, or even the *Enterprise* herself.

"The City on the Edge of Forever": (Kirk falls in love with a woman who must die or else the entire future will be changed.)

A lot of people think this was the best show we ever did. I never read the original script that Harlan Ellison wrote. He was very upset with what they did with it. I've learned that since then. Actually, Scotty's involvement in the script's original draft was widely misreported. Gene told people that the script had Scotty dealing drugs, and although I didn't see that first script, my understanding is that that is definitely not the case. Unfortunately it was reported that way, repeatedly.

Harlan didn't like his show being cut up. If you ask me, the only way to have really done justice to his original script would have been to do it as a film. Perhaps he had similar feelings; certainly he felt that what wound up on the screen wasn't representative of what he'd originally conceived. Even though he has diarrhea of the mouth, I really like Harlan; he's a smart son of a gun. I like some of the things he says and dislike some of the others.

"Operation: Annihilate": (Kirk's brother is killed by creatures that look like flying omelets.)

Those things went hurtling through the air on strings, and

when the script called for one of them to smack Spock in the back, it nearly knocked him down.

That episode was filmed at a very modern building down where TRW has its offices—in Torrance or somewhere south of Los Angeles International Airport.

They had satellites—I think they were communications satellites—that I was allowed to see while we were filming there. The people in the room with them were wearing outfits that looked like space costumes so that they wouldn't drop anything into the works—completely covered, with gloves on. There was no dust at all allowed in that space, which is why it's called a "clean room." From outside it you saw these people working, and robots, too.

"Catspaw": (Haunted castles, a sorceress, and weird magicians. Halloween in the future.)

One of the few times I got nailed in the blooper reels, because "One-Take" Doohan needed *a couple of takes* in a scene where I'm supposed to walk down a short flight of stairs. There I was in a dimly lit set, staring straight ahead in a zombie-ized, catatonic state, holding a phaser, and navigating the stairs.

Now, granted, actors have to develop good peripheral vision. We have to be able to hit our marks, know where to stop, know how to move, without looking down at our feet in a distracting manner. But on this occasion I just couldn't see a damned thing.

"Metamorphosis": (Kirk, Spock, McCoy, and an ailing Starfleet official come upon a long-believed-dead scientist and the cloud creature who loves him.)

According to an earlier draft, Scotty was included in the shuttle crew. The engineer would have enjoyed talking shop with Cochrane, the missing scientist. Plus it was Scotty who got zapped by the companion and, together with Mr. Spock, constructed the device that would have short-circuited the entity. In short, I would have had a ton to do in that episode, at least as much as I had in "The Galileo Seven." I was up to thirteen episodes at that time, and I have no idea why I was cut out of that one so much. Instead, my part was divvied up between Spock and Kirk.

"Friday's Child": (Kirk, Spock, and McCoy get caught up in a tribal dispute, which results in their kidnapping the pregnant widow of the tribal ruler.)

An offbeat piece of casting it was to have Julie Newmar as Eleen, a nine-months-pregnant woman. Julie has always been aggressively proud of her figure and remains so to this day. In fact, at one Creation Convention, she marched around in a one-piece bathing suit to show the crowd that there wasn't an ounce of fat on her. The crowd was suitably impressed.

This is one of the many episodes where Kirk ignored the Prime Directive, that means noninterference, after all. If Kirk hadn't interfered, Eleen (who had been ready to die after her husband was killed) would have been executed, and that would have been that. Instead, he disobeyed regs and got himself, and two of his senior officers, into a world of trouble.

Behaving in far more commendable fashion (I like to think) was his chief engineer, left in command of the ship, which was always a fun thing to be. I thought I ran the ship beautifully, to tell the truth. It was a nice change of pace, although I think Scotty's best place was in the engine room. It was in this episode that Scotty uttered the much quoted line, "Fool me once, shame on you . . . Fool me twice, shame on me." There's also a bit of sloppy continuity in the teaser, as Lieutenant Josephs (James Mitchell) switches sides of the screen in relation to Kirk in different angles. Those kinds of mistakes are inevitable in the weekly grind of getting a television series out.

I wonder, though, how today's audience would handle McCoy's rather unsympathetic treatment of Eleen. When he places his hand on her belly, she slaps him . . . and McCoy slugs her back. He later tells Kirk that he's going to be keeping that little maneuver in his medical repertoire for future need. I can just see the fans reacting to that: "Did you see last night's episode? McCoy slaps women around! What a brute!"

"Who Mourns for Adonais?": (The *Enterprise* is menaced by a being claiming to be the Greek god Apollo.)

This episode brought us Leslie Parrish. She was absolutely lovely, and I can tell you that a lot of sticky glue went into keeping her costume together. I met her on the show and dated her a couple of times. There was just something about her. She was a charming dinner companion, absolutely gorgeous, but she knew how to break down and be a good talker. There were no airs to her at all.

She told me, "Gracious, in early movies, there were parts I played where I opened my mouth and put my foot in it with my accent." She really had had to learn how to talk non-Ozark hillbilly. Although, of course, when she played Daisy Mae in *Li'l Abner,* her Ozark leanings probably served her rather well.

This was also a memorable episode to me for the stunt work I got to do when Apollo "zapped" me with a bolt of lightning. I had a harness on under my red shirt, with a highly tensile wire held by a couple of stunt men. They pulled me back when he zapped me. I practically flew backward, and if there hadn't been other stunt guys there to catch me, I might've gone through a back wall. Following that shot there's another one of me on the ground, after the stunt men have moved off and disconnected the harness.

I had to talk them into letting me to do the fly-back. I said, "I can do that! Why not let me do that? That's pretty damned safe." It was more fun for me, and certainly mild in comparison to other stuff I'd done. In Canada, we'd once filmed a sequence where I was on a train moving eighteen miles per hour, and I rolled out of a train car and did somersaults down an embankment. That was a piece of cake. I got a few scratches, that's all.

* * *

141

"The Doomsday Machine": (The *Enterprise* battles a huge, planet-killing robot.)

One of my favorite episodes, written by Norman Spinrad in very scientific terms. It was highly suspenseful, down to the last second.

The Jefferies tube was not the most comfortable of sets to work in. It was a tube with a hole in the top, and the tube was set at an angle of fifteen degrees from the perpendicular. When Scotty goes leaping up the Jefferies tube to try to fix the malfunctioning transporter, he mutters a curse. People ask me what I was saying, and I hate to disappoint them, but it was just something along the lines of "Bragus blath"—a made-up Scottish curse. I knew Scotty had to express his impatience *somehow,* and that seemed the best way to do it.

According to Alan Asherman, lost for one brief line of dialogue in this episode was Scotty's brogue: "Thirty seconds later, poof!" is supposedly spoken without the famous Aberdeen accent. To that, I have to say: Picky picky picky.

"Wolf in the Fold": (Scotty is the prime suspect in a series of grisly murders that turn out to have been committed by a newly returned Jack the Ripper.)

At least I got a chance to do some acting, something a bit beyond, "Cap'n, I canna change the laws of physics!" Here was Scotty being threatened, having to protect himself, but he didn't know how. I thought, "Thank God, they're doing something with me, giving me something to do, because I'm tired of doing just one thing."

It also gave me a chance to work with my old friend, Johnny Fiedler (playing Mr. Hengist, a fussy administrator type who turns out to be the murderer).

Watching, with a broad grin, the dancing girl was no great stunt. In fact, I dated Tanya Lamani, who played the exotic dancing girl, a few times. Tanya, who was a tiny woman, was the best belly dancer in town. Did all her dancing barefoot, like Martha Graham, and used to dance at a Greek restaurant on Hollywood Boulevard. We'd go for long drives out to a restaurant in Malibu. Last time I saw her, she was seeing a guy who was, in my opinion, as good a dancer as Fred Astaire or Gene Kelly.

Scotty had the line, "You don't have to tell an old Aberdeen pub crawler how to applaud." The line was a tip of the hat from the producers to my having told them about the Aberdonian who was the basis for the accent.

During one sequence, Scotty is being questioned in connection with the murders. The script calls for me to have my right hand flat on a lit pad that scans my life signs and indicates whether I'm telling the truth or not. Right hand. A problem because of the missing you-know-what. So during that sequence I cheated a bit. I kept my hand forward and my fingers curled under the edge so that the AWOL digit wasn't obvious. And at one point, there's an insert close-up on the hand. Notice the long, tapering, graceful fingers of Montgomery Scott . . . all five of them. It was a mutually amicable decision. Director Joe Pevney had no desire to risk throwing a viewer mentally out of the scene with a startled, "Hey, look, Scotty's missing a finger!" I, as always, preferred to keep it out of the limelight. So we had a stunt hand step in for Scotty.

As much as I loved that script, there were some . . . interesting aspects to it. Such as the concept that the entity targeted women because apparently, all through the galaxy, females were more easily terrified. I wouldn't say that's necessarily the case even on this planet, much less a galactic constant.

And then there was Kirk's odd strategy when the entity took over the *Enterprise* computer and started laughing madly in an effort to frighten the crew and feed off their emotion. Rather than trusting the crew to deal with the entity in a calm, professional manner, Kirk decided to have McCoy pump every single crew member (with the heroic exception of himself, of course, and the emotionally challenged Spock) full of tranquilizers. He doped his people up rather than count on their training to see them through.

Finally, when the entity has been dispatched, Captain

Kirk—without missing a beat—immediately tries to talk Spock into beaming down to the planet with him to check out a "place" with women so amazing that words are never found to describe them. Think about it: Kirk wants to leave his ship in the hands of 430 drunk drivers (Sulu is literally spinning in his chair) so he can go planetside and score. Kirk ultimately discards the idea, probably because he remembers that he has a ship full of a hundred or so females, all with great legs, miniskirts, and all of whom will be in an *extremely* good mood for, according to McCoy, the next five hours. Why go out when you can order in?

"The Changeling": (The *Enterprise* encounters a sentient, perfection-seeking probe called Nomad, which threatens to "sterilize," i.e., kill, everyone on the ship.)

So there I was, reading the script, and I get to the end of the second act. It's always important that the second act break be as strong as possible, because that's the half-hour mark and you want to make sure you hold on to the viewer into the next half hour.

Well, they'd picked a doozy of an act ender this time.

Dr. McCoy looks up from a red-shirted individual. He's just given one of his customary detailed examinations, which consists of checking for a pulse and that's pretty much it. (McCoy wasn't much for crash carts or heroic attempts to save a downed crewman.) And he speaks to Kirk that most dreaded of lines: "He's dead, Jim."

What chilled my blood was that the person wearing the red shirt this time was Scotty, apparently having been killed after a futile attempt to pull Uhura from Nomad's clutches.

Now, I had been signed for six more episodes. Nonetheless, that was a real heart-stopper. Why hadn't anyone said anything to me? Were they planning to? Were they going to call my agent?

Slowly I turned the page to the top of act three, in hopes that Scotty would suddenly sit up, blinking and saying,

"You're a little premature this time, Doctor." But no, Scotty was still dead. Kirk was upset. Things weren't looking good.

And then I got to the part where Nomad's asking Kirk whether repairs should be effected on "the unit Scott." I heard a hoarse sound and realized that it was my breath finally being released. I wasn't dead. I was a plot twist.

Of course, I can chuckle about it now. In fact, at *Star Trek* conventions I describe how Scotty was lying there, flooded with an absolutely clear, brilliant light at the gates of heaven. Only one final test to get into heaven awaits me. And suddenly here comes DeForest Kelley with his salt and pepper shakers to make me better. I wake up, the glories of heaven lost, and think, "Same old place."

Ah, well. Better that place than unemployment, I guess.

There was one early sequence on the bridge where Kirk is talking to Nomad in preparation for beaming him aboard. During one take, Bill dropped out an entire line in which he asks whether Nomad will require any specialized adjustment in the ship's environment (unaware that Nomad is a machine through and through). Knowing the take would be unusable, I stepped into frame on cue, and, instead of saying my own line, I said, "But, Captain, you're forgetting about the environment . . . and all that stuff. Are you sure you really want to do that?" and then walked back out of frame as Bill grinned and shook his head, realizing that he'd screwed up his own line. That sequence is on the blooper reels.

"Mirror, Mirror": (Kirk, Scotty, McCoy, and Uhura get tossed into a parallel and somewhat barbaric alternate version of the *Enterprise*.)

Leonard looked very good with a beard—but, being Vulcan, why did it have to come straight down like that? Of course, he's half human, but they could have had it different, sticking out from the sides.

Nichelle had a new two-piece outfit for that one—a little vest and a skirt that slanted upward. There were quite a few appreciative glances, not to mention whistles, the first time she came out of her dressing room in *that* ensemble.

This is the one and only episode where I dramatically address the captain as "Jim!" when it looks as if he might be left behind in the mirror universe. Quite a change in attitude from "The Doomsday Machine" when I left him aboard the *Constellation,* which I'd just rigged into a giant bomb. There I just gave a fairly sanguine, "Good luck, Captain," and I was out of there. Guess Scotty became more fond of Kirk somewhere between the two.

"The Deadly Years": (Kirk, Spock, McCoy, and Scotty age at a precipitous rate.)

Remember how I told you I was in and out of makeup, under ordinary circumstances, in ten minutes? Not this time. First, I had to wrinkle my face up and then they'd put stuff on my skin to maintain the wrinkles, even when I subsequently relaxed my face. I was in the chair for about three and a half hours. When people used to ask me if I wanted to be in *Star Trek: The Next Generation,* I'd say, "Hell, no." Not if it meant having to be aged, the way they did with DeForest in "Encounter at Farpoint." He didn't have one square centimeter of his face without at least five wrinkles in it. And I certainly had had more than enough of that from this episode alone.

They didn't give me any lines during most of the sequences, which is why I sat there looking forlorn and deflated: "As if somebody had cut the strings on a marionette," as one text commented. But you have to look the part.

"The Trouble with Tribbles": (Fast-multiplying furry creatures threaten to overwhelm the ship.)

This episode probably did the most since "Wolf in the Fold" to establish Scotty's character and dynamics. That was a lot of fun. I had a nice scene in the bar with the Klingons, and I had to hush Chekov—and before you knew it, I was the one doing the stuff Kirk didn't want.

I loved the scene where Kirk is trying to figure out if Scotty started the fight over love of his captain and it turns out that the far more important insult involved the ship. How dare they!

It's the only episode I can think of where Scotty has the last line, namely, "Where they'll be no tribble at all." That was my version of the last line, which was actually, "Where they'll be no trouble at all." I didn't tell them I was going to say it that way; I just slipped it into one of the takes. And they wound up using it.

Actors will often come up with memorable bits of business or line tweaks. For example, when I was saying to Korax the Klingon, "Laddie, don't ye think ye should . . . rephrase that," Michael Pataki, who played Korax, came up with the notion of imitating my brogue when he responds, "Ye're right, ah should."

I did about ninety-five percent of my own stunts in the big fight scene. About five percent, they used a stunt man, where some flying through the air was involved. It took about two hours to film the whole fight, once everything was lit. It was still a lot of fun to do. My stunt double, Jay Jones, said to me, when I had done all this stuff, "If I ever become famous, would you be my stunt man?"

All in all, David Gerrold wrote a very solid script. Although he had a good deal of help, both from Gene and from Dorothy C. Fontana, who started out as Gene's secretary and became a hell of a writer in her own right. David's an odd one, though. There was a while there where rumors were all over the place that I had died, and it turned out that David was always making an announcement at conventions, like once a year, announcing, "Oh, Scotty died." It was meant as a joke I suppose, but the rumors *really* got to be a bit much. I (proving my continued existence by the shrewd expedient of walking out onto the stage) finally told the fans, "Will you quit listening to someone who doesn't know what they're talking about? I'm very healthy."

* * *

"By Any Other Name": (The *Enterprise* is hijacked by aliens, most of the crew is turned into dodecahedrons, and the remaining crew members fight back by introducing the aliens to the inconveniences of their human forms.)

Most people remember me from the scene where I'm drinking Robert Fortier, who played Tomar, under the table. One exchange quickly became famous. Scotty produces yet another bottle of booze and Tomar says, "What is it?" The somewhat soused Scotty studies it and then shrugs and says, "It's . . . It's green."

In fact, it became such a noted line, that when I guest-starred on *Star Trek: The Next Generation,* Ron Moore wrote a scene between Scotty and Data in which Data makes the same pronouncement about yet another bottle of alcohol.

Bob Fortier and I weren't really drinking alcohol, of course. It was colored water, being consumed at eight in the morning. By nine-thirty in the morning, I started to slip down the wall and they called, "Cut!" And I looked up and said, "Anybody got any real scotch?"

Sandy Meisner had spoken of the twenty-year journey in acting, remember, but thanks to the circumstances under which I'd grown up, I sure didn't need any twenty years to be able to act the way a drunk behaves. I'd observed it firsthand for far too long. I play a very good drunk.

Back in my live-television days in Toronto, there was one occasion when I played a RCMP (Royal Canadian Mounted Police) undercover officer in a bar. Kate Reid, a wonderful Canadian actress (later in *The Andromeda Strain),* was in it with me.

About forty-five minutes before we were to go on the air, I was lying on a narrow bench, floating in the alpha state of utter relaxation—that form of meditation and inner reflection achieved through careful breathing and mental discipline—which my mother had likewise been able to achieve. I didn't do it all the time, but it was particularly useful when embarking on a challenging stage role. I was running through the show in my head. The director and the rest of the cast came in, and the director started giving notes. I just lay there, taking in what he was saying, giving barely perceptible nods. All Kate saw was that I was lying there. Two minutes before airtime I hauled myself up and saw the way Kate was looking at me, and immediately said in a voice bordering on drunken stupor, "How ya doin', Kate?"

Panicked because we're about to go on live, Kate blurts, "Jimmy, you had too much to drink!"

"Nonshensh, Kate, I can hold m'liquor . . ."

I don't think a single red blood cell remained in her face as we closed on to twenty seconds before airtime, at which point I suddenly snapped to normal and said, "How ya doin', honey?"

She wasn't sure whether she should just be grateful or strangle me.

"Return to Tomorrow": (Several disembodied aliens take over the bodies of several crew members, and trouble results.)

As mentioned earlier, I did the voice of the lead alien, Sargon. They can do practically anything with your voice— stretch it, compact it, take out the highs or lows. They mostly manage that; you can't give yourself credit for that sort of stuff. Sargon was much lower than I normally speak, but they did that all electronically.

This episode also featured Diana Muldaur, who not only would return in our third season, but also became a regular for one season on *The Next Generation.* Some mutual acquaintances had a party at which I met Diana. She made one hell of an impression. The rest of the *Star Trek* cast was there as well, seated at one end of three long tables. Walter, De, George, Nichelle, and maybe Leonard were there, and Bill was at the other end of the table propositioning Diana. We know because we all heard her say, "Oh, you little man. If I wanted to fuck anybody, it'd be Jimmy Doohan."

Give Bill a crazy kind of credit for the fact that he gets

himself into situations like that and it's water off a duck's back. He says these things, gets slapped down, and it's as if it never happened.

I ran into Diana more recently on a *Star Trek* cruise, and she said to me, "Remember that day?"

And I said, "I have loved you ever since."

"Patterns of Force": (A world where a Nazi society rules, thanks to interference by a Starfleet offical.)

Seeing actors in the Nazi costumes brought back thoughts of the war, naturally. But when you get right down to it, I saw only two Nazis in my life, the two soldiers in the church tower that I shot at during the Normandy invasion. It was nighttime when I was wounded, so I never saw my assailant. So, the only others I saw were the "Nazis" on the screen in somebody else's movies.

During this episode, all I could think was how gullible the German people were. They were suckered into Hitler—and some of them loved it. There will always be those who appeal to the worst instincts in humanity.

"Assignment: Earth": (In the 1960s, our heroes encounter a mysterious man named Gary Seven [Robert Lansing] who may or may not be out to start World War III.)

I remember Robert Lansing when he was a regular guy, hanging out at Cromwell's drugstore in New York. When I got to Hollywood, he had already done *12 O'Clock High* and a few other series. And I remember I thought, *My god, this isn't the guy from Cromwell's,* because he was so hoity-toity with me. I didn't mess around with him much because I hate that sort of phony stuff.

The first two seasons of *Star Trek* had their ups and downs, but as we rolled into the third season and endured Gene's departure (more on that later), it was a lot more downs than ups.

* * *

"Spock's Brain": (Spock's brain is stolen by a race of women.)

Many fans consider this rock-bottom *Star Trek,* and I tend to agree—although some have said it was almost worth it because of the parody it spawned twenty years later on *The Wonder Years,* with young Fred Savage doing a perfect Kirk impression.

What a lousy one this was. Freddy Freiberger had no idea what he was doing. He was just a line producer, suddenly handed creative control over a show that was like nothing else on television. There was no blueprint for him, no way for Freiberger to guide himself. A lot of fans seem to place the blame for the third season on Freiberger, but it wasn't entirely his fault. He was simply out of his depth, and, boy, was that loudly announced to the fans with this episode.

"Spectre of the Gun": (Shoot-out at an alien reconstruction of the OK Corral.)

This was kind of interesting, I thought. Kind of fun and well done, too. It's the only time Scotty does a mind-meld with Spock. I tried to have Scotty look extremely creeped out by the thing. His thinking was along the lines of, "Don't mess with me." Nobody in their right mind wants somebody to see them in their wrong mind.

"Elaan of Troyius": (Kirk has to "tame a shrew," an uncivilized woman who has to marry an alien ruler in order for their two planets to achieve peace.)

Another one of *Star Trek*'s rather odd commentaries on feminism. Elaan, as played by France Nuyen, is a tough-minded, independent-spirited woman who ultimately is browbeaten into accepting a marriage thrust upon her against her will. And this is what Kirk is working *toward.* Kirk lectures her at length about responsibility and following orders, which is somewhat amusing coming from a guy who flaunts the rules and bucks orders whenever it suits him.

France was a sweetheart of a woman. She had several

different costumes, including one with colored glass on it that I thought was one of the best ever. France and I used to sit for hours and hours as she'd tell me about her love life with Robert Culp.

There's one bit of odd editing in this episode involving Scotty. In one scene in engineering, Kirk orders Elaan to thank Scotty for giving her a tour of the room. Elaan turns and looks at the expectant engineer. They decided that they wanted to cut in a close-up of Scotty looking down at her, waiting for Elaan's gratitude. But John Meredyth Lucas, who both wrote and directed this episode, hadn't shot any "coverage" that showed Scotty doing that. So they cut in a close-up from later on in that episode—specifically, from a scene where Scotty is about to inform Kirk of the death of a crewman. As a result, the lighting and Scotty's expression in the "death" close-up are totally inconsistent with that of the "gratitude" master shot. Not only that, in the "death of a crewman" sequence there's a security man standing against a far wall, a man who isn't there in the master shot of the "gratitude" scene. So in that first scene he winds up just appearing and then disappearing again. Ah, those *Enterprise* security men can be a tricky lot.

"And the Children Shall Lead": ("The Turn of the Screw" in *Star Trek* terms, with kids worshipping a "friendly angel" played by attorney Melvin Belli.)

Melvin Belli didn't know how to act. How in the hell did he ever get in that job? I don't know. Was he someone's friend or something. This is the sort of thing went on in the third year, when Gene wasn't looking after things.

"Day of the Dove": (An entity that feeds on hatred pits the crew against an invading group of Klingons.)

I wonder if the entity that fed off hatred was any sort of relative to the entity that fed off fear back in "Wolf in the Fold." If so, they must have had interesting family reunions.

As the entity influenced us more and more, we had to act

bigger and bigger, notching up the intensity as much as we could. It's fun every so often to act in a manner so completely contrary to character, although as the histrionics level rose, we all started sounding dangerously like Kirk did normally.

I also had a great time wielding the claymore. Why should George have had all the fun, after all? It was the only episode in which Scotty got to do any swashbuckling.

I'd had some training in stage fencing during my days at the Playhouse. Not a good deal, mind you, about five or six hours all together. Stage fencing isn't the same as sport fencing. In the latter, the object is to try and strike at particular points on your opponent. Sport-fencing engagements are rapid engagements of parry and thrust before a touch is made. The object of stage or theatrical fencing is twofold. First, quite simply, you want to look good. The engagements are lengthy, minutes at a time in some instances, carefully choreographed. The key is to be totally in synch with your partner, which brings me to the second object of stage fencing—not losing an eye. Sport fencers are covered with all manner of protective gear, while stage fencing requires you to be wearing only whatever your character's costume is. One mistake, one assumption that your partner's blade is going to be in one place when it turns out to be five inches to the right, and an unfortunate accident can be the reward.

The sword fights themselves could have had better sound effects. Oddly, in the big Klingon versus *Enterprise* climactic battle between the crews, the sounds are more akin to swords slamming on shields than blade against blade. There's no way for me to check this after all this time, but it sounds as if they used the same SFX (sound effects) as from "Bread and Circuses."

There's a really nice trading card that depicts Scotty going into the armory and finding the wall of swords. Thirty years ago, who knew that we'd be on trading cards? We just thought we'd be lucky if we made it to a fourth season, which of course we didn't.

* * *

"Let That Be Your Last Battlefield": (An allegory about prejudice as two two-toned beings—played by Frank Gorshin and Lou Antonio—battle it out for no good reason except bigotry.)

Aside from the production crew having to clean Frank's teethmarks off the scenery (but, oh, no one chewed scenery like Gorshin), I liked that episode. Prejudice is, at its core, stupid, and I thought this was an outstanding demonstration of that. The crew wear looks of incredulity when Bele (Gorshin) explains that the inferiority of his opponent Lokai (Antonio) stems from the fact that Bele is black on his right side while Lokai is white on his right side. This is all the "proof" that Bele needs for his belief that Lokai is inferior.

It seems so utterly absurd . . . until one considers that "Battlefield" is only a slight tilt away from the reality of prejudice in our society. To say nothing of situations such as Bosnia, where people have been slaughtering each other for centuries over belief systems.

Gene always conceived *Star Trek* to be, at its best, a means of making commentary on the real world. By cloaking it as science fiction, it made the "lesson" more palatable. "Battlefield" might have been a bit heavy-handed in its presentation, but the message was a solid one.

"The Way to Eden": (Space hippies take over the *Enterprise.*)

Well, the description really does say it all, doesn't it?

It's often said that the caliber of a story's hero is directly connected to the caliber of the villain who opposes him. It's one thing when Khan and his supermen seize control of the *Enterprise;* that was seventy-plus genetically engineered individuals who were, left to their own devices, capable of taking over planet Earth. You could respect bad guys such as they.

But *these* guys? Hollywood's idea of hippies, taking command of a ship with 430 highly trained Starfleet professionals? Jamming with Mr. Spock? Given free rein to wander about the ship rather than being confined? How much patience could Kirk realistically have had with these fools? He should have slapped them in the brig and left them to rot the moment they all shouted "Herbert" at him. The fact that one of them was the son of some ambassador should have cut no ice with Kirk. He certainly had no hesitation in telling ambassadors where to go in person, much less the obnoxious son of one.

It was going to be a godawful show, and I could tell from the moment I read the script. I started making inquiries to the producers about the possibility of my opting out of that one, but I let them convince me that it might actually be a fun, offbeat episode—social commentary on the generation gap.

I should've gone with my instincts.

"The Savage Curtain": (A rocklike alien creates a good versus evil drama by pitting Kirk and Spock, along with Abraham Lincoln and several others, against villains from the past.)

This was the only episode in which we see Scotty in a kilt. I loved to put the kilt on.

As the film *Braveheart* made unquestionably clear for all time, Scotsmen basically wear nothing under their kilts. But I did. There was a young lady who was a visitor to the set at the time and tried to find out what I had on. I told her she couldn't, because there were other folks around. But, I suggested, how about if we go back to my dressing room . . .?

I didn't expect her to have the nerve to take me up on it, and she didn't.

"The Lights of Zetar": (Sentient flashes of light take over the body of newcomer Mira Romaine.)

It was nice to have an episode that focused on Scotty, although his fixation on Mira Romaine certainly seemed to come out of nowhere. The fixation was more of a matter of plot convenience, to give the episode more emotional depth, rather than something that flowed naturally out of Scotty's personality. On the other hand, it also gave them yet another chance to zap poor Scotty, who always seemed to get his head handed to him whenever he tried to save a crewwoman in distress (see "The Changeling" and "Who Mourns for Adonais?").

"Turnabout Intruder": (Kirk's personality is exchanged with that of a demented woman scientist.)

Our last episode, and believe me we *knew* it was our last episode. The mood was not an upbeat one. We had gotten our third season through the herculean efforts of the fans, and then the fans were let down through the combination of sorry stories and our lousy time slot.

Still, we did our best with this last one, and, you know, there were some nice scenes for Scotty, particularly the moment when Scotty schemes with McCoy to take over the ship since the captain is literally out of his head.

What was odd in this episode was the implication that women couldn't possibly be starship captains. Then again, it was just one of many odd things that occurred in the third season's scripts.

14

Family Album

THE *STAR TREK* FAMILY OF ACTORS AND CREATORS, LIKE ANY family, had its ups and down. There were those I felt closer to, those I felt further from. For better or worse, other people tended to think of us as a unit.

George Takei and I got along like a house on fire. If we were working late on a Friday, he and I would go down to Tokyo Kaikan, which was the only Japanese restaurant in the city at the time, or at least the biggest one, and I got to like sushi, because it went so well with scotch. We'd go down and sit at the bar; George would drink wine, I think. We'd have a good time doing that. Now George has found a sushi restaurant called Ike's (pronounced EE-KAY) on the corner of Gower and Hollywood Boulevard, and we go there all the time.

I always had a lot of fun with George. He was complaining about his Jaguar once, and I said, "Let me hear the engine run." Then I pulled out the oil stick, and, God, he needed three quarts of oil! So the standing joke for me is, "George, have you checked your oil lately?"

When Walter Koenig first came aboard the show during the first part of the second season, he was very nervous. Poor

Walter—he's a dour Russian. As he gets to know you, *that's* when he becomes depressed. Walter always feels as if he's a third cousin, instead of a real first cousin. Still, I don't think many people realize how funny Walter can be, with his dry sense of humor and quick wit—what a combination. He is also an excellent writer, and it's too bad that talent wasn't tapped during the original series (although he did contribute a script to the animated series).

I thought bringing Walter on board was a great idea. It was only right to have a Russian in there. To me, the whole idea was to have a great mixture of accents, to emphasize the international flavor of the series. And considering that Bill, De, Nichelle, and George had fairly straightforward, North American accents, it was nice to have that Russian accent breaking things up.

Gene really liked DeForest Kelley. Who wouldn't? I think DeForest was scheduled for the show and couldn't do it, but then when the pilot was sold, he could do it. Gene was very impressed with DeForest and liked him an awful lot.

Nichelle Nichols was, to me, part of the series to add to the international look of *Star Trek,* to have a black person, a Scottish person, an Asian person. Nichelle wasn't given much to do. I always thought that was too bad, because I understand she had quite a bit of experience on the stage in musicals. "Hailing frequencies open, sir" doesn't embody much of a character.

Perhaps that's why she would be late coming onto the set. *"What am I going to do today? Say 'Hailing frequencies open' again."*

Leonard Nimoy, now, he was just a terrific person. Aside from his being a wonderful actor—although it's getting ahead of things a bit—I want to say he was also the best director we ever had, without a doubt. He had all his homework done. He had the photographer's homework done; he had the scene designer's homework done; and, if you weren't careful, he'd have your homework done, too.

It's very simple. Leonard didn't talk for five minutes about what he wanted a scene to do. He just told you, "It's just like so-and-so and so-and-so," all in a couple of sentences. All good directors do that. Any really good director can tell you what he wants in a few phrases.

I felt no trepidation at all when I first heard that Leonard would be directing *Star Trek III: The Search for Spock.* I knew Leonard—he would think of the show first, rather than himself.

As for Bill Shatner, well . . . I have to admit, I just don't like the man. And, as has been well-documented elsewhere, he didn't exactly have a knack for generating good feelings about him.

It's a shame that he wasn't secure enough in himself or his status to refrain from practicing that sort of behavior.

Yet he was oblivious of the effect he had on people, as became clear in the way he recounted in one of his books his encounter with Nichelle, letting him know that much of the rest of the cast harbored hostility toward him.

Overseeing it all was our creator, Gene Roddenberry. At heart, Gene was simply a television producer who wanted to get a television series on the air and was willing to listen to everyone and anyone who could make it a better series.

By the same token, Gene was very much "hands-on," particularly during the first two seasons. He was in control, even in the second year, when Gene Coon had taken on the day to day stuff. Gene Roddenberry was still doing the politicking with Paramount and NBC, fighting for the integrity of the show and his vision of it.

Gene, to me, was not a great writer, but, boy, did he know how to help a writer become somebody. He would help them along, and he could definitely spot talent. It was a "do as I say, not as I do" sort of thing. His secretary, for instance, was Dorothy Fontana. Dorothy already had some television scripts to her credit, having been freelancing on the side. She came up with ideas for shows, and Gene said, "Sit down and write it." And when she started turning out shows like "Charlie X" and "Tomorrow Is Yesterday," not to mention her rewrite on "This Side of Paradise," she eventually became story editor. Gene may have been short on talent, but he certainly could exploit it in others—and that's "exploit" in the most positive sense.

It has been said that in subsequent years, as *Star Trek*'s popularity increased, Gene was stingy about doling out credit where credit was due. I think there's some truth to that. But I think that one of Gene's great qualities was that an ordinary idea would come in for a show and he would turn it into something better. His own scripts were never anywhere near as good as the other ones. You knew it was Gene who pushed the writer to make it better. That's where Gene's great talent was, in saying to a fellow, "Why don't you do this, why don't you do that? You have to have a conflict," and so on. The writer would become successful just by following Gene's instructions.

But Gene couldn't do it for himself. The shows he wrote were never nearly as good as, shall we say, Gene Coon's.

Gene Coon came aboard midway through the first season as a writer-producer and penned some of the series' most memorable episodes. You'd go to Gene Coon's place for dinner, and just talking before dinner was served, he'd give you three ideas for movies that he had thought of that day. You'd be knocked out by it. If you'd had the money, or the ability to produce and get the money, you would have done every damned movie he ever thought of. He made it sound so fabulous, so easy. He just thought them up as easily as you'd snap your fingers. Gene Coon was a marvelous, marvelous man.

Although Gene Coon died of lung cancer, I remember Gene Roddenberry saying to me once, sometime after Coon died, "Yeah, he died of a broken heart." His girlfriend, his childhood sweetheart, whom he had married, didn't turn out as well when he married her. She didn't love him as much as he'd hoped. Gene said that's what broke his heart.

The point is, if you don't keep up the fight, you can become depressed, and, all of a sudden, you're gone. People allow sickness to enter their bodies just by being depressed about something.

And speaking of depressed . . .

As hands-on as Gene was during the first two seasons, he was completely hands-off for the third, and it showed. To me, the third year's failure was absolutely and totally Gene Roddenberry's responsibility. He was not there to control things, and I was incredibly angry about it at the time. We had to do shows that were little more than words strung together, with no help, no shaping of a vision by someone who *had* vision. Gene used to correct and correct and correct other scripts, but when it came down to the third year . . .

It was around this time that I actually began to socialize with Gene, because I was going out with his then secretary, Anita. Anita was very much on her own during that time, because Gene was so upset about the third year—"under duress," shall we say—that he wasn't in the office three, four, five weeks in a row. A script would come in, and he would never even look at it. Anita didn't talk about it much, but she was just sitting around an empty office taking messages. It was boring for her, since the boss never came in.

By the time Gene and I really started to become close, the show had ended, and I certainly was not reticent about telling him my opinions about the way he had abandoned the series. I told him many times, "You should have stuck to your guns and done your proper work. It's like a carpenter not joining two pieces of wood in the proper way. Crap is a hell of a legacy to leave behind."

He'd mumble, "Paramount just mistreated me." But I said then, and say now, that that was no cause for bad work.

In 1970 I married Anita. Gene and Majel Barrett, Anita and I, became something of a foursome. There were long periods of time when they were at our house three nights a week, and we were at their house three nights a week. We started playing bridge with them. Anita was a very good bridge player, as were Gene and Majel. I wasn't, but I learned from them.

In addition to bridge, Gene and I also shot pool a good deal, on a pool table of mine that I wound up selling to him. I've got tremendous peripheral vision, and out of the corner of my eye I'd see Gene moving the ball closer to the pocket. And I'd say, "Gene, what are you doing?! This is for *twenty-five cents!*" He didn't like to lose, not even a quarter.

Gene and I had one thing in particular in common—a love of aviation. As any good longtime *Star Trek* fan knows, Gene Roddenberry had also been a pilot in his younger days. He would regale me with stories of his flying days, his particular favorite being an incident during his time as a Pan Am pilot. He would fly from Constantinople to New Delhi, or Egypt to New Delhi.

There was one time where he crash-landed in an Arabian desert. Two clichés come to mind. The first being that any landing that you can walk away from is a good one. However, when that calls for you to "walk away" into the middle of a desert, you've definitely wandered from the frying pan into the fire.

Then Gene had a stroke of luck; he was quickly found by an Arab sheik. Now, this might lead you to think that Gene promptly found himself in the midst of hedonistic revelry. Belly dancers, harems, and whatever other erotica you've seen in those old desert epics.

But not Gene, no. No, he had the luck to be picked up by an Arab sheik with an exceedingly effeminate manner. Yes, a pronouncedly gay sheik, who started making romantic overtures to Gene. This was a hell of a situation for Gene. How does one turn down a come-on from a guy who could—if he takes offense—leave you to die in a barren wasteland? Talk about being caught between Iraq and a hard place.

Having no desire to boldly go where, apparently, other men had gone before, Gene did turn down the sheik. The sheik was not thrilled to have his overtures rebuffed, but at least he didn't take too great umbrage over it. If he had, I doubt we would have ever heard from Gene Roddenberry again.

Gene and I also did a good bit of sailboating. He and I went out one time to the Santa Barbara area, to the Channel Islands, and got permission to sleep on a big private island called Santa Rosa. We set up a grill on the sand, talked about our early days, and generally had a great time. I would say that Gene was at his best when he was away from the pressures of the production office. Then again, who *isn't* a bit more relaxed when removed from the stress of the daily grind.

But when we woke up the next morning, we were surrounded by fog so thick that though Gene was sitting four feet away, he might as well have been four hundred feet away.

We hadn't anticipated any problem with the return trip, because without fog the far shore was clearly visible. As it was, we were completely blinded. But undaunted, Gene said, "Jimmy, I'll tell you what. I'll plot a course, you get it ready to move, and I'll give you a heading."

I had some trepidation over the fact that we were sailing entirely on a heading that Gene was calculating from his own skull, but nonetheless I went along with it. And an hour later, we were no more than forty yards off Santa Barbara Harbor.

There was a second trip sometime later, where we went out with a one-knot wind blowing. Just before we left, I suggested we fill up the gas tank, but Gene said briskly, "Nah, we're fine. Start up the engine and let's go." So we put the sails down, started the engine, and headed for Avalon out on Santa Catalina Island. We figured to be back at about two in the afternoon.

And wouldn't you know, half an hour later the engine quit.

Up went the sail again, and with that pathetic one-knot wind propelling us, we limped in at about nine-thirty at night. I was there the next morning when Gene had a mechanic flown in from San Pedro on a seaplane. The mechanic started checking out the engine, took about five seconds, and announced, "You're out of gas."

Gene wouldn't even look me in the eye. I said, sounding innocent as anything, "Was it not having enough gas that caused you to crash in the desert?" He *claimed* it wasn't.

Great navigator, but a lousy engineer.

There was another time that the four of us hit very, very rough water going up toward the Channel Islands, up off of Ana Capa. Somehow, Gene lost his watch. He whispered to me, "I've lost my watch; don't tell Majel." And I said, "Okay." We were heeled over and we were taking down more and more sail. It was getting to be a gale.

Six weeks later, he found the watch. It had rolled under the scuppers somewhere. And it was still ticking.

Majel was at our house when Gene proposed to her. We were living in Burbank at the time, right near the Warner Brothers Studios in Toluca Lake.

Anita and I were sitting in the dining room, and Majel was on the kitchen phone, just sitting there, happy, with the tears streaming down her face. She was just crying and smiling like you can't believe. The tears were just streaming down her face, she was so happy.

Gene was in Japan, you see, and Majel had come over for dinner and to play Liverpool gin rummy. It was probably about ten o'clock at night. Japan time, it was into the next day, maybe nine or ten hours difference. Gene wanted her to fly to Japan to get married. She was just bubbling all over the place. I remember asking her when she left the house a half hour later, "Are you sure you will be okay driving home?" And she said, "I'll calm down, I'll calm down."

We told her the stuff she needed, like a passport, because I don't think she had one. We told her, "You'll have to fly through Anchorage, connect with Gene, tell him when you're coming . . . but go to a travel agent." I promote travel agents because I hate those people who are standing in front of me on a line at an airport, haven't been to a travel agent, and make the airport ticket clerk do the whole damn thing for them. It doesn't cost a thing to use a travel agent.

And she wound up going to Japan, where she and Gene were married in a lovely Shinto wedding ceremony.

Despite all the talk of philosophy that *Star Trek* spawned, Gene was not especially philosophical or a great thinker of deep thoughts. But when the show took off, the fans flocked to the "Great Bird of the Galaxy," asking him to lay eggs of wisdom on them, and he was concerned about ending up with egg on his face. Everyone from the fans to the press asked him what had given the show its cachet, and poor Gene was fumbling around trying to find words to describe it. He was rather shocked by the reaction to the show, I think. He was not a good public speaker, not particularly expressive about his deepest thoughts, whatever those might have been. He couldn't use words the way a philosopher could.

He spent the next years of his life trying to remake himself in the image that the fans had cast. I really don't think he had expected what had happened. I don't think he had expected his show to take off like that; I think he was a little dumbfounded.

All of us were, really. Remember, all we had on our hands was a three-season show that had never done particularly well in the ratings. Yet it did well enough to overshadow many of our careers, and seemingly became an albatross around our neck when it came to finding more work.

None of us could have known just how far the albatross would actually fly . . .

15

Star Stuck

HOLLYWOOD HAS SUCH A TYPE-CASTING MENTALITY. CASTING directors and the Hollywood business world think only in terms of, "He can do this and nothing else." That's the way it happens. I used to do every other kind of accent; I did a Scottish accent only once before *Star Trek,* in one episode of *Hazel.*

In fact, the director of the second pilot, Jim Goldstone, used me for about nine other shows after that, and he'd say, "What accent can we use today?" Paul Wilkins, my agent at the time, would just say to me, "He wants you there," and he'd ask what accent we could use. I did a Lancashire accent, or Russian or French. I had so many roles before *Star Trek,* and I always tried to look different in each one. I never suspected I'd be typecast, because I always tried to look different.

When the series ended, there was the normal sadness that goes with the end of any such . . . enterprise. You're leaving people you've been working with, whom you've come to think of as a family. By the same token, as I mentioned earlier, the third season of *Star Trek* was a miserable situation because of the types of scripts they were giving us. At least I was out of that uninspiring, visionless environment. Sure, I was unemployed, but that's a normal state of affairs for actors. It didn't even occur to me that the acquisition of jobs, which had come so easily to me before, was suddenly going to become a hardship.

It hardly seemed fair. All of a sudden I found myself saddled with all the disadvantages of a popular series (namely, being locked into a particular characterization) and none of the advantages (namely, continued employment). To make matters worse, my marriage to Anita disintegrated—fortunately there were no children—and I found myself having to try to rebuild both my personal and professional life. It was a toss-up which was going to be more difficult.

Not that there was *no* work after *Star Trek.* For instance, I was in an episode of *Then Came Bronson,* which involved the nomadic adventures of the titular hero (played by Michael Parks), whose preferred means of locomotion was a motorcycle. The series was produced by *Star Trek* alumni Herb Solow and Robert Justman.

The script called for me to ride on the back of the motorcycle with Parks doing the driving. It quickly became clear to me that he hadn't had much experience with a motorcycle. I'm purely speculating here, but if he was a typical actor, when he was being considered for the part and was asked about motorcycle riding, he said, "Of course I can ride a motorcycle! I'm an old hand at it." I don't know why anyone ever bothers to ask actors about special skills, because the same thing will happen every time: the actor will claim expertise, and then—if he gets the part—will quickly run out and try to learn it.

In any event, the riding sequences were going somewhat wobbly. I was doing my job to stay balanced, but he wasn't doing his very well. He tried to blame it on me, demanding, "Have you ever ridden a motorcycle before?"

"Yeah, about sixty thousand miles during the war," I shot back.

To his credit, he quickly apologized. "Oh, shit, I'm sorry. I haven't driven much on motorcycle," he admitted in a slightly lowered voice.

Naturally I became conciliatory. "You're doing okay," I said. "We haven't fallen, have we? Then don't worry about it."

I did a couple of movies. One was a film that Gene Roddenberry was producing with Rock Hudson called *Pretty Maids All in a Row.* It was about Hudson being a teacher in a high school and humping all these girls . . . and so they wouldn't tell, he killed them. It was a murder mystery, also starring Angie Dickinson, with Roger Vadim directing. Vadim spent days taking pictures of four or five young girls walking up and down stairways, so that their breasts would bounce up and down.

I got the job because Gene Coon suggested to Gene Roddenberry that he hire Bill Campbell, and then added, "While you're at it, Jimmy Doohan's a friend of Bill's; why not hire him, too?" I wound up getting the better part.

A director I had worked for in 1962—Richard Sarafian—called me up from Madrid in January 1971, and said, "Jimmy, can you do a French-Canadian accent?" I said I could, he said, "You're hired; be over here in five days, and let your beard grow." I was over there in about three days, and I worked over there for five months on the movie, which was called *Man in the Wilderness.* It starred Richard Harris and was a darned good movie, although you hardly ever see me in it.

But more often than not, I'd encounter the frustration of landing a part because I was known as Scotty. I was hired for *Magnum, P.I.,* with Tom Selleck, and didn't realize they wanted a Scotsman. I started to do the line readings, and they said, "Where's the accent?" I *really* didn't like that.

I thought of Sandy Meisner's comment about a twenty-year journey. It seemed that the road I'd been traveling on that journey had abruptly been sidetracked. I'd been knocked off the high road onto the low road, leading inevitably to the not-so-bonnie bonnie banks of typecasting.

But Aaron Spelling hired me for *Fantasy Island,* and he hired me because I'm an actor. He didn't hire me because of Scotty. Another time I was on *Hotel* for him; he just said, "You can do whatever you want to do. If you want to use an accent, go ahead, but you don't have to be a Scotsman."

Still, television episodic work was few and far between, and I needed to pay the bills. I retreated to my first love, the stage, landing in a production in late 1973 in San Francisco called *The Trial of James McNeill Whistler.* I got rave notices playing a *veddy* proper British barrister, circa 1885. It involved an art critic named John Ruskin who wrote some vicious things about artist James Whistler (known for, among other things, immortalizing his mother in a portrait). I was Whistler's barrister, pushing the case for him. It was a case in which Whistler won a moral victory, but as a practical matter, he lost, because John Ruskin was fined all of a farthing.

During one performance in early 1974, two young (and I do mean young) ladies came backstage to get autographs. One was named Julie, and she'd brought a friend, Wende. Julie had made a gift of the ticket to Wende, because Wende was a big fan of Scotty's.

I couldn't take my eyes off Wende. Quickly I did the autographs, but I said, "I don't have any pictures, but if you'll send me your address, I'll send you some." Naturally, I had a healthy stock of pictures handy, but, hey, what other way was there to get her address?

She wrote me a nice note, and I called her back saying, "Would you like to come to see the play again?"

Afterward, we went to Enrico's on Broadway in San Francisco, to have a drink. It was a fairly romantic place. Although some parts of it were lively, we had a nice quiet little corner. We were having a nice get-to-know-you conversation, when several other cast members arrived, shouting, "Hey, look!

Jimmy's got a table already!" And our quiet corner got very noisy.

I invited her again to see the show, and again we went to Enrico's. Wende had her hair down, and she was wearing a light blue dress. She was the epitome of beauty to me. Absolutely perfect. She had such a smile, and when I kissed her, she had the smoothest, most luscious lips in the world. She still does; it would knock you out. I think it was that second evening that I proposed to her. I said, "Honey, I'd love to have you marry me. You don't have to say yes or no for quite a long while, if that's what it takes. I will wait."

It was a cool night as we walked from the restaurant, holding hands, over to my car. I had a little Volvo 1800E at the time.

Time passed and she hadn't said anything. I wasn't nervous about it. She was just my gal, and that was that.

We saw each other as much as we could, since she had moved up to Petaluma to live with her girlfriend. When we didn't see each other, we wrote letters. In fact, a lot of our courtship was through the mail.

When the play ended, around the first of September, I stayed in Petaluma for a short while. We became officially engaged before I had to return to Los Angeles. There I found that my grass had grown by about five feet. I'd let out the house to a young kid from San Francisco with the proviso that he look after the lawn. Well, he did plenty of looking. Just no maintenance. I had a gorgeous lemon tree that gave about two or three thousand lemons a year, and they would plop down onto that huge carpet of grass and bounce right back up again, without even getting bruised.

Wende finished tying up loose ends, borrowed a van, and drove to Los Angeles. That was a quick turnaround, since she had to return the van and fly back down before I left for England for an appearance. We got married just three days after I returned, on October 12, 1974.

It was a small ceremony, in the chapel right around the corner from my house. In fact, William (Bill) Campbell (yes,

Trelane and Koloth from "Squire of Gothos" and "The Trouble With Tribbles," respectively) was my best man. We had a reception back at our house, which is where we left the guests while Bill and his wife took us out to dinner. Imagine our surprise when we returned to find that all the guests had stayed. Rudy Solari, who had played Whistler in San Francisco, was regaling everyone with his stories, and, God rest his soul, what a storyteller he was. Fortunately (for those who stayed, that is), I had a ton of my famous white lasagna in the fridge, so we were able to feed everybody before pushing them out the door.

We took a honeymoon up to Vancouver. It was Wende's first train ride across the Canadian Rockies, which are unbelievably beautiful. They're not really visible from the road. We went to Calgary and stayed there a couple of days. The Charging Rivers there are something else. The Thompson River and the Fraser; you'd go out of your mind just seeing them.

So now I was a married man once more, looking to start another family . . . with bills to pay that would probably only get larger and an acting career that wasn't burgeoning.

Meantime, however, *Star Trek* fandom was swelling larger and larger . . . and, much to my surprise, providing a means of making ends meet.

16

Fan Dancing

YOU HAVE TO UNDERSTAND, IN SHOW BUSINESS, ACTORS ARE treated, as Alfred Hitchcock once said, like cattle. Condescended to, handled as if we were slabs of meat.

So it's something of a shock to find yourself up on stage in a ballroom—a packed ballroom, mind you—with fans hanging on your every word. It's a heady, gratifying experience. For someone who's in a business that specializes in tearing you down, it's certainly a welcome change to be faced with eager young people who build you up.

It started for me with an outfit called the Program Corporation of America. They wrote me a letter that said they were getting a lot of calls. People were interested in me, wanting to know if I would like to go to universities and get a good fee for doing it. That was in 1972. The Program Corporation took a fee of thirty percent, but the remaining seventy was money I wouldn't have had otherwise. It looked like a nice way to be carried through dry times. It made sense. If *Star Trek* was going to constrict my acting career, at least it was giving something back as well.

I went to a community college in upstate New York when I

was doing the college tours. Over the course of seven years I went to at least 250 colleges and universities, all separate invitations, no sort of organized tour.

I turned down hardly any invitations. I accepted everything. That was my living at the time; I was typecast, not getting jobs. It was a godsend, really.

At first I didn't know what to do with the fans. No clue. There was a Canadian fellow named Larry Mann out in Hollywood who used to write material for Lorne Greene. I told Mann I'd like some funny one-liners about *Star Trek* to start out my appearances with. I wanted to get some laughs. About three weeks later he called me and said, "Your stuff's ready."

I went there, picked it up, and started reading it. He had about ten or twelve pages of minute-and-a-half stories, some of which I knew already . . . including one about a Scotsman.

"I asked for one-liners," I said.

"Well, these are what I do."

"But that's not what I paid for."

I didn't know what to do. I was out $2,500. A year or two later, somebody referred to "your friend, Larry Mann," and I said, "He's no friend of mine."

The first *Star Trek* convention was held in 1972 in New York at the Commodore Hotel. Organized by a group who called themselves The Committee, it was a spectacular success and gave *Star Trek* fandom nationwide exposure . . . particularly when it received coverage in *TV Guide.* Gene was a guest at the first one and was utterly stunned by the devotion of the fans to what was—insofar as any of us knew—simply a canceled television show. As if there weren't thousands of them littering the landscape of television history.

My first *Star Trek* convention was the following year, at the Commodore. When I was first contacted about attending, it was a question of, "I want airfare—coach—and a hotel room paid for. And I want to be picked up at the airport." That was it. I don't think I charged much beyond a minimal appearance fee, if that.

I had heard that three thousand people turned up for Gene at the first convention, so I expected about the same amount. And I think that was about right.

I stood on the stage in the grand ballroom of the Commodore for my first appearance, looking out at what had to be over a thousand eager faces. The feeling it gave me can't be described. It was my first real inkling of the power of *Star Trek,* of what the series meant to them, of what Scotty meant to them. They wanted so much from me, they wanted so much for me to live up to whatever preconceptions they'd put upon me, and I wasn't sure at first what to do. How to make the connection that I knew they wanted.

After fielding initial questions about myself, about Scotty, and about *Star Trek,* the answer came to me in what was an impulsive act which—nonetheless—felt right. I suddenly announced to the crowd, "Okay, I'm coming down there now to shake hands with every single one of you." And before the explosive roar was even fully realized, I jumped down off the stage into the midst of the audience.

From the corner of my eye, I saw one of the convention security guards go ashen, shouting into a walkie-talkie, "Jimmy just got off the stage and started wading into the audience!" The voice of convention organizer Stu Hellinger was heard over the walkie-talkie moaning, *"Ohhhh,* my Goddddd . . ."

Obviously the concern was that they were going to rip me to shreds. But I knew that wasn't going to be the case. This was a lovefest, a celebration of the joy that *Star Trek* brought to fans, and as I worked the crowd I gave them exactly what they wanted and all they really needed—that moment of connection.

Still, concern about a frenzied reaction of hysteria reared its head once more when it turned out that Leonard was going to be able to make the convention.

Oh, there were rumors rampant throughout the weekend,

but no one knew for sure he was going to be there. He was intended as a surprise guest.

When he showed up, they brought him up through the press room, where he fielded questions from reporters and various publications. The press room was packed solid, with journalists jockeying for position. One aggressive photographer leapfrogged all the way from the back of the room to the front just to get a decent photo. Then Leonard was ushered out through various back entrances and service corridors.

If the fans had known he was already there, about to step out on stage, there might have been who-knows-what happening. With the rumors of Leonard's possible appearance at fever pitch, people were running around trying to find him or stampeding to get to the front just in case. Sure, my earlier foray into the audience had been greeted with restraint, but my move was sudden and unexpected. Leonard's anticipated appearance was gaining the speed and strength of a locomotive that could have run us all over.

With the rumors going wild, it was decided that I would defuse them. I went out on stage and told the packed house, "I have a special announcement to make. Leonard Nimoy . . . is on his way to the hotel."

A cheer went up, applause . . . thunderous. With the rumor reported as true, it couldn't spiral any further out of control. And since everyone now "knew" that Leonard wasn't there yet, things were a bit calmer.

There was no little video room, as would be common in later conventions. Instead they ran sixteen-millimeter films on movie screens in the grand ballroom. In this instance, everyone sat and watched *Silent Running,* although silent it wasn't. There was a constant buzz of anticipation. And then they stopped the film, and Leonard came out. I thought the applause would never stop.

I can remember that I was the guy who started autograph sessions, and all the other cast members were pissed off at me for doing that. But they went along with it . . . most of the time. For instance, once Bill and I were doing a big car show in Denver called "A World of Wheels." I was up on the platform autographing for a big line of people, and Bill was way down at the other end. I was signing for hour upon hour, while Bill was handing out prestamped autographed pictures.

Sometimes my hand cramps up, particularly if I autograph for more than an hour and a half.

I autographed at a video store on a Paramount promotion—in Long View, Washington, on the Columbia River—and I made the store stay open. They were concerned about the overtime and all, and I said, "Hey, these are your future customers."

As the years passed, fans would even come to me at conventions with pictures they'd taken five years ago, standing beside me, and they'd get those autographed.

In the early days I personalized my autographs, signing them, "To So-and-So." I don't do that anymore, except on rare occasions, and I usually have to limit autographs to one per person. Sometimes fans give elaborate sob stories. There's "My son had to leave early," or someone coming on behalf of an alleged person in the hospital: "Oh, they're very, very sick, but they'd love to have your autograph." And I'd have to say, "I'm sorry, but there are no exceptions—one autograph, that's it." Now I have people who sit beside me and check everything. They are the people who refuse things, so I don't have to be the bad guy, refusing to personalize or sign more than one.

Plus, the autographed pictures can fetch significant sums of money on the secondary market. There have been signed pictures of me in memorabilia shops from Disney World to Newark, New Jersey, all going for hundreds of dollars. The point is, it's more valuable to you in the future for a photo not to be personalized—because who wants your personalization on something? Suppose you die? Your children can keep the photo if they want, or sell it if it just says "James Doohan" on it.

Some actors feel that when they give an autograph, they're

doing the fan a favor. But I've had them packed in the doorway, and the way I look at it, they're doing me a favor.

In Charleston, West Virginia, they told me there was damn near a riot at the Creation Convention because they had to tell people the place was jam-packed and turn them away. I felt sorry that these people weren't able to get in. If I had been told earlier, if somebody had said, "Jimmy, we've got a problem . . ." I might have done another session.

I didn't like people to go away without something. So usually I said, "We'll just sit down and I'll sign things." And I'd do it till the very end—except in places where we knew darn well there were absolutely too many people. Like the big one in Chicago in 1975 with sixteen thousand people. That was the first really big one. Everybody in the show was there as a guest. We did one the following February, in 1976, run by the same girl, Lisa Boynton. It was in New York and was so badly oversold that it was shut down by the fire marshals. It was ten degrees above zero, and there were five thousand people waiting outside for the next show, trying to keep themselves warm.

The amount of knowledge the fans have about the series is simply amazing. The fans know every darn line of the show. One of the conventions runs a game called "Name that Episode." I would do a line of dialogue, and the fans had to guess which episode. And they were fantastic. The Midwest is the best. You can't fool an audience in the Midwest.

Once I appeared on a morning television show in Pittsburgh, and they didn't tell me they were going to have a trivia quiz. This didn't bode well, because I don't remember much of anything. They asked me three questions, and damned if I didn't know the answers. I couldn't believe it. I looked like a bloody genius. Of course, not all the questions or discussions at conventions centered on trivia. Some of the typical questions were:

"What's Mr. Spock like?" Not Leonard Nimoy, but Spock.

I would tell them that Leonard is one heck of a guy, just a terrific person—and they'd be satisfied with that.

"How does the transporter work?" Well, the real answer of course is that we stand on these little circles of light, they run the camera, they put the lights on and off as we stand there about thirty seconds. Then we step off and they run the camera for about thirty seconds. Then they edit it by using your picture once every five times, every ten times, etc., and before you know it, you're out or you're in. Of course, now it's different and all done by computers—much simpler and cheaper because they don't have to send it away to the optical people to have the sparkles put on.

But the fans frequently want to know scientific answers for how things in the *Star Trek* universe work. How do the engines work, how do the phasers work?

It's like the fact that after three hundred years have gone by, we've learned to control antimatter. As a matter of fact, after *Star Trek* was on, antimatter was discovered and put into a magnet, and it still, to this day, is flitting around inside a magnet in Switzerland. All they had to do is control it. A spark of power from matter meeting antimatter would make a hydrogen bomb look like a candle. We would have unlimited power in this world if we could do that.

The science right now is seventy-five years ahead of the economy. In the case of many inventions, there is no point in even thinking of, working on, or bringing them into public use, because the economy is not ready for them.

So I would try and come up with answers to all the fans' questions, because that's what they expected.

The bottom line is, they expect you to do whatever you possibly can.

We knew a girl in Kentucky named Laura Scarsdale, who told us about a badly injured deputy sheriff. He'd delivered an eviction notice to someone who took great offense and accosted the sheriff, beat him, shot him, and left him for dead. The deputy sheriff had been laid up for quite a while.

Laura asked me to call him in the hospital, and I said, "Sure, that's no big deal."

You talk for fifteen or twenty seconds to somebody, and a little blood pumps a little better, a little faster. That sort of thing has happened, and Laura, of course, absolutely adored the fact that I'd do that.

Some fans come prepared with something they want to say. Some of them give me letters that I obviously don't read until on the way home. Sometimes I have a little pile of things on the autograph table that I have to take away with me. One fan down in Melbourne, Florida, gave me a book by astronaut Deke Slayton. That was very interesting to read.

Unfortunately, sometimes they give me something fragile, made out of glass or somesuch. Some things are so big you cannot carry them onto the plane, and the notion of trusting them to baggage handlers is a terrifying one.

Once I went to a community college in northern Georgia, just south of Chattanooga (the latter being a great rail center, by the way, with model trains all over). I got to the college about noon, and they said, "You're going to show the blooper reels; can we check them out first?" They didn't use the word "censor," but that's what they were trying to do, make sure that it was suitable material for . . . whomever. I thought that was a little strange.

I was introduced at four and did an autographing session that lasted until seven. A woman brought in a five-by-nine foot painting of all the *Star Trek* people. I'd like to say it was nice looking, but . . . it wasn't. From her conversation, it was evident she wanted me to take it home.

Rather than spend a couple of hundred dollars to pack the thing up, I said, "You know, you should really give this to the public library. They would adore it!" And she said, "What a marvelous idea!" And before she could change her mind, I was out of there inside of twenty seconds.

I had a fan, a young lady in Chicago, who did a wonderful little cartoon of me sitting in a chair, asleep, with the radio saying, "Beam me up, Scotty." I went to her and asked, "Could I buy that from you for a hundred and fifty dollars and use it?" She said, "Sure."

What did I use them for? Magnets.

What I'd do is, if people were nice to me, did something special for me, I'd give them a magnet with that illustration printed on it. I travel with United Airlines the majority of the time—that and Delta—and when they started with the frequent-flyer program, they made it better for me. The hostess, host, captain, and crew of United planes are the biggest group of recipients of these magnets. I'm now into my fourth batch of five thousand of them—and I've warned people that in the future I'm going to start selling them autographed. This last batch, I signed two thousand five hundred of them on St. Patrick's Day, with green ink.

I got in touch with the artist later and said I'd give her five percent of the five thousand magnets, which would be two hundred and fifty. She got those, and I have another five thousand . . . and I've lost her address. She's somewhere in Indianapolis now. I'll save the two hundred and fifty for her.

Everything in life has its positives and negatives, and certainly *Star Trek* fans are no exception. But I can tell you that the negatives of *Star Trek* fans are becoming less and less because, for some reason or other, it's become such a big love affair.

There are the occasional dangerous situations. Once was in Boston, when they actually found a guy with a weapon on him, all dressed in camouflage clothes. Somebody saw the gun on him, and he was asking for me. But the police were brought in, and they took him away.

Then there was a guy in Orlando. He wasn't really threatening-looking, but you can never tell for sure. He found ways to get onto my floor in the hotel, into special places where I was doing interviews. How he knew where I was, I have no idea—but he knew, and he tried to force his way in. Finally, we called security.

I read of celebrity stalkers and such, but I'm not too

worried. Basically, I know how to handle myself. Not that I'm anywhere near as strong or as quick as I used to be, but I know how to do things—I had six weeks of commando training. It doesn't make me a full commando or anything, but it was a gorgeous part of my officer training in England.

Years ago, the James Doohan Fan Club was organized. It began when Anna Hreha came up to me on the set because she was into fandom. She said, "Would you like me to organize a fan club for you?"

I asked, "What do I have to do?"

She said, "Maybe four times a year you write what you're doing, your activities and stuff. Basically, that's it. Sign some things like, 'You are now an official member of the James Doohan Fan Club.'"

Anna now lives in Seattle, her husband having passed away just before she turned sixty-five. She had had another girl become the president of the company/fan club. When that girl moved down to Texas or something, Anna took over. Anna runs a fan club like nobody else runs a fan club; it was the best there was. Hundreds of fans would say she is just marvelous. There are still people who send letters to me through Anna; she just readdresses and sends them on to me.

The club's no longer active. We were at a convention in Kansas City once, and she came: "You know, Jimmy, I think we're going to have to do something with the fan club—because I'll be traveling a lot and going to university and trying to fill my life up with nice things. Do we want to look for someone else to run it?"

I said, "No, nobody will run it like you did, Anna. You are the best, and the fans tell me that. We've been together for all this time, and there have been no complaints from anybody." So we decided to stop the fan club altogether.

During the original series, I used to get about fifteen to twenty letters a week. Now it's up to forty or fifty a week; it keeps piling up, and I just can't handle it anymore. I don't want anybody else to do it, and I admit I have four signature stamps waiting for sometime when my hand might not be up for signing.

I thought maybe I should get my writing hand fixed, because it kept cramping up. I went to a doctor in Los Angeles and said, "Can you fix that?" He took X rays and said, "Yes. In ten years the knuckles may get twice as big, and then I will have to do something." With the thought of that, I made the autograph into rubber stamps, just in case. At least I would be the one rubber-stamping it.

I consider fandom a sort of huge, extended family. It's a marvelous kind of thing, yet I know people who look on the fans—for some reason—as trash. Actors who say, "Who in the hell wants to sit down with a bunch of bums?" I'm not going to say who said it, but when I hear people say things like that, I immediately dislike them.

Sometimes fans try to convert me; a lot of Jehovah's Witnesses will drop stuff off. Fans will ask me, "Are you a Christian?" And I say, "Yes." Then they give me a tract from the Bible. Hey, I'm Catholic; I've had it in spades.

The extent of fan interaction I can manage depends on how many people there are in any given situation. We used to be able to interact with them a lot more, before the crowds got so big. You just can't personalize anymore (although George manages to do it somehow).

And then there are some of the truly odd aspects of fandom. For example, so I've been told: pornographic comic strips of all of us, even one between Kirk and Spock—I'm always with some girl. But I've never actually seen them. Fans say, "Oh, yeah, I have one," and I say, "Why don't you copy it and send me one?" But they never do.

Probably the single oddest fan was one I encountered in the Americana Hotel on Seventh Avenue in New York at a convention about twenty years back. This fellow came up to me as I was standing with some "civilians," shall we say, waiting for an elevator to take me up to my room. He was a young teenager, about fourteen, medium height. Sandy-haired, not blond, eager, seemed quite bright. He said, "Mr. Scott . . . can I get a sample of your blood?"

He brought out this little kit that he had. Staring at it worriedly, I said, "Hey, son, I'd only go for a blood test if it was under the purest of medical conditions."

"Oh, I've already done two hundred and fifty. I have two hundred and fifty different people's blood," he said cheerfully. The civilians were standing by, gaping.

The elevator picked that moment to show up, and I said hurriedly, "Excuse me, son, I've got to go." I got into the elevator, the other people clustering around me. The door closed, leaving the disappointed fan behind, and the civilians said, "He wanted your *blood?*"

About six years later, I was going to colleges, and this guy came up to me. He was lighter-haired and six feet tall, and he said, "I'm the guy who wanted to have a sample of your blood in the Americana Hotel in New York."

I said, "My God."

He said, "Can I get it now?"

That's too much.

A *Star Trek* convention in New Haven, about nine years ago, resulted in a most unexpected reunion.

Shortly before going to the convention, I'd been speaking with an old friend, Howie Cameron, a noted bone surgeon in London, Ontario. When I say "old" I'm not exaggerating. Back in my high school days, if Kay and I were on the outs, Howie would get a date with her and take her out. There was one Sadie Hawkins dance where Howie made sure that Kay was there to witness the gorgeous redhead from Port Huron who'd brought me to the dance. Made Kay nuts. Got us back together, in fact.

Anyway, I was talking to Howie, and he said, "Jimmy, you know, if you're going to be in New Haven . . . Kay's living in Danbury, Connecticut, now. And her husband, Joe . . . he's been dead for three years. Why don't you call her up?"

I was extremely hesitant. It had been nearly forty years, after all. To say nothing of how a married man's wife might react to the prospect of her husband calling on an old girlfriend.

But Wende is a confident and secure enough woman that she doesn't feel threatened by such a prospect. She urged me to look her up as well.

So there I was in New Haven, about forty minutes away from Danbury, and I called her up and said, "Kay . . . this is Jimmy Doohan."

She said, "Oh, my God . . . wait'll I sit down."

I said, "Look, how about brunch tomorrow, Sunday."

"That would be marvelous!"

She gave me directions on how to get to her house, and then called me back a half hour later to tell me that she'd given me the wrong directions and had to correct them. The next day I traveled the winding road to her home nearby Candlewood Lake. You know the old saying that if you want to see what the daughter will look like in the future, look at the mother? Well, I think Kay looked just the way her mother would have if I'd met her mother twenty years later than I did. I parked the car, and she was just standing in the doorway. And I just opened my arms, and she came running to me, and we just hugged and hugged.

My God, Kay and I couldn't stop talking, just going on and on with everything that had happened in our lives, what had been before, and what was this and what was that, and what was anything else and how was this related to that. We had an eleven-thirty reservation for brunch and got so caught up in talking that we didn't get there until one in the afternoon.

And there, at the brunch, as we discussed our last date back in Port Huron, when I told her I had thought she considered the romance over, she made it equally clear that I had completely misread her.

"Jimmy," she said, "all you had to do was just say, 'Kay . . . why don't we try again and see how it goes?' All you had to do was say that."

I was flabbergasted. I said, "Kay, I had no idea what I was going to do with my life at the time. And you were already set! And you had somebody else who was already set."

I was astounded to learn that she had also voiced that sentiment to my sister, Margaret. The two of them had become quite close in those days. One time Kay had pointed to a gate and said, "If Jimmy and Joe came through that gate at the same time, I know who I'd go to. It would be Jimmy."

And Margaret never breathed a word of it.

Between the two of them, you'd have thought that *someone* might have mentioned *something* about it to me. There I was squarely in the driver's seat, and I—unknowingly—had kept the damned car in neutral. People claim that women can't keep a secret. Well, they certainly can . . . just at the worst times.

I've seen Kay from time to time since then. Give me credit for knowing that Joe Cherry offered her a life with tremendous prospects. She's very well off, with a big condominium down in Fort Lauderdale. Rodney Dangerfield lives below her on the twenty-sixth floor; she lives on the twenty-seventh.

Trust me to find out that I was right . . . and still feel uninformed at the same time.

17

The Continuing Voyages

ABOUT THE SAME TIME THAT I BEGAN MY FORAY INTO FANDOM, *Star Trek* launched into its next incarnation: animation.

Word went out throughout fandom that the *Star Trek* animated series was going to be something major. A quantum leap in visualization of *Trek* adventures. Sure, we'd be trimmed down to half-hour episodes, but in animation there was no limit to the possibilities of visual effects. Anything that a script writer could come up with that an animator could draw would be fair game. The potential seemed endless and exciting.

I was down at California State University at Long Beach— I don't recall why—and Leonard was down there. I had heard that Leonard had told Paramount that he would not do the animated shows if Nichelle and George were not included. Paramount wanted to drop them from the show to save money. And Leonard, who had the clout to do so, told Paramount, "You put them in, or I don't do the show." That's the kind of guy Leonard is. And they were kept in, and that made everybody except the Paramount bean counters happy.

In that respect, Leonard is much like Spock, because Spock

would never let that sort of thing happen, either. But Leonard's not one to make a scene about it. He's contained. If he doesn't want to do something, he doesn't do it.

The animated series was, in a way, rather fun for me because I have the facility for doing them. I tried for no accents at all in the animated series as I performed ancillary characters. I tried to do it with just changes of voice and speed, or slowness of speaking. There was a new alien character named Arrex, the navigator, to whom I gave voice. If I could manage to do more than three characters in an episode, they had to double my pay. So that was always kind of fun, to see how many characters I could do in the thing. I think that I did ten of them with four voices, so that was double pay. One of them, I did five voices.

They never had the cast all together to do them. All they did was take our voices, take our characters to the animators, and do it page by page. We did the tapings once a week up near the corner of Sherman Way, outside of Hollywood.

I didn't even have someone reading the other characters for me to play off of. I was just reading my lines. It wasn't all that difficult for me; I had done that kind of stuff so much that it was just a piece of cake for me.

But I wasn't pleased with how the animated series turned out. It was too dull, without much action. Characters were static, barely moving, nor did the likenesses look much like any of us. Certainly mine didn't.

At that point I never thought that *Star Trek* would come back in any way, shape, or form. It was quite evident to me that they were just going to do the animated series to make a little money. My guess is that Gene spearheaded it. He talked up the animated series because he wasn't getting much action out of Paramount executives, who seemed absolutely dead when it came down to the concept of reviving *Star Trek*. But the other series that Gene tried to get rolling simply didn't go anywhere. They didn't have the blessing that *Star Trek* had for him.

*   *   *

A couple of years before the *Star Trek* movies got off the ground, there were all sorts of rumors flying around. Well, I heard something from somebody that was obviously just a rumor, but I wondered to myself, "Maybe I should call Bill." I wasn't getting straight answers from anyone else and thought maybe he'd be in the know. I finally called, and I got right through to him, which was very unusual. He generally has someone else take the call, and then he'll decide if he'll talk to you or not. But I got right through, and I said, "Hi, Bill, this is Jimmy Doohan."

And he was furious that I had called him. "How'd you get my telephone number?!" he demanded angrily.

I immediately hung up. The hell with him.

There was an abortive attempt at a second series. And while they were working on the script, it kind of changed my life completely. Wende and I had been planning to get the hell out of Los Angeles, and we were at the point of going out to take a look at some property at a price that we could handle. There were some really good-size properties, with nice houses on them, in the San Francisco, Sacramento area, and also near the coast.

All of a sudden we got a call from my agent saying, "Hey, we're going to do a series." Now, I rather liked the idea. The problem was, if they had been only going to do a movie, we could have gotten out of Los Angeles. But if it was a series, we had to stay put. And we were saying, "Oh, God," because we wanted to get out of the creepy little house that Wende and I were living in.

Paramount had difficulty deciding whether *Star Trek* should be a feature or a series. And once they decided on a television series, we reluctantly started looking for another house in the area.

So they started working on the script for the first episode, and guess what? They started saying, "Well, hey, jeez, this might turn into a movie."

We had signed a contract for a series, and, with no

compensation at all, they suddenly changed it to a movie. Wende and I had already moved into the new house, which we hated, to accommodate the series that wasn't going to be.

The first moment when I stepped onto the set of *Star Trek: The Motion Picture* was an amazing one. They brought me over to the set for the engine room and lit it up for me to inspect. It was breathtaking. It made me think of the dinky engine room that I had worked in during the first season and, for that matter, the notion to eliminate the part of the engineer and the engine room altogether. How far we had come.

Filming *Star Trek: The Motion Picture* was okay, except that they signed a contract with a guy for special effects who didn't seem to know what he was doing. Once the studio had seen what he had done they had to bring in Doug Trumbull because the original effects were not acceptable.

People ask me what it was like for the cast to be together again. In a large way, we'd never really been apart. It hadn't been like most television shows where the series is cancelled and you all go your separate ways to new jobs, and the show simply goes on your résumé. Many of us hadn't gone on to new jobs (at least not with enough frequency to suit us), and how "separate" could we be considering that we were seeing each other at conventions all the time?

So, I wasn't overwhelmed with a sense of sentimentality. If anything, I was happy that we were finally going to be making a living out of Paramount. After years of limbo, suddenly the success of *Star Wars* and *Close Encounters* had gotten their attention. They were coming to us and paying us movie-size salaries to resuscitate *Star Trek.* It was quite a sense of validation.

The pace of making films is startlingly, amazingly slow in comparison to television. It all has to do with the lighting. On television, the shots are designed for a small screen, and you can get away with a great deal of cheating in lighting a scene. Block the scene, string up some lights, bring the actors in and shoot that sucker. Get an hour show out every week. Theoretically, if you shot a movie the same way, every film would be done in two week's time, maximum.

Instead, shooting schedules take eight, ten, twelve, fourteen weeks. An incredible amount of care and detail is poured into every frame of a motion picture, because the big screen is *very* unforgiving of the slightest production gaffes.

Plus, the more leisurely pace could make for superior performances (providing, of course, you have a solid director at the helm). When filming television, there's a basic attitude that says, "Okay, we got it, let's move on." That it could be better isn't as important as the fact that it's good enough. It was nice to be able to apply the disciplines of theatrical films to *Star Trek.*

This was one of those occasions where having "Scotty" in the family made a major difference, because the twins— Montgomery and Chris—were in the movie as extras.

The costumes in the first film were incredibly ugly. They weren't even particularly functional. I had to run a few times and, guess what? My feet came out of my boots, which were sewn into the uniform. Three years of original *Star Trek* on a budget that was a fragment of what they tossed into *The Motion Picture,* and I can assure you that when I ran in my old uniform, by gosh my feet stayed where they were supposed to be. Boy, was that stupidly designed. They must have known that people would have to do other things in the movie uniforms than walk carefully.

Who decided that the film should hit the theaters on December 7 of 1980? December 7, the anniversary of the bombing of Pearl Harbor. That's always when you want to open a film, on the anniversary of one of the biggest bombings in the country's history. Why give reviewers a straight line like that? To say nothing of the ill-advised promotional line for the film, "There's no comparison." Some fans came out of the first showing shaking their heads and muttering, "There's no comparison," as they reminisced over how exciting the original series was in comparison to that snorer.

Well . . . I might as well admit it. I fell asleep at the

premiere (and I understand that Bill did, also). Although I survived the interminable "once more around the *Enterprise*" sequence earlier in the film, they lost me with the ship's approach to V'Ger. Who in the world needed to spend ten to twelve minutes getting to V'Ger with silvery-looking clouds and wisps of air and fog? I heard the film was nicknamed, *Star Trek: The Motionless Picture,* and with good reason. My wife was elbowing me and saying, "C'mon, wake up." Believe me, my dozing wasn't scotch-induced. I was just bored.

Star Trek II: The Wrath of Khan was a somewhat better experience. Nicholas Meyer, the director, was just a gem as far as I was concerned.

They found out that Harve Bennett was a successful series producer and had done a few films. They called him in and asked, "What did you think of *Star Trek: The Motion Picture?*"

And Bennett said, "Too slow."

They asked, "Can you produce a movie for twelve million dollars?" And he said, "Certainly."

Why the drop in budget? Because obviously the studio bigwigs had blown their top at the cost of the first one and were out to cut the waste.

I have to give Harve Bennett credit. He sat down and started watching *Star Trek* episodes. A couple in the morning, a couple more in the afternoon. He sat there in the private screening room and became a *Star Trek* fan.

Finally, he decided that the episode he could get the best movie out of was "Space Seed" with Ricardo Montalban. The thing was, of course, that the possibility of doing a sequel to "Space Seed" hinged entirely on getting Ricardo. (Although, y'know, Jack Palance might have been interesting. . . .)

Obviously, Ricardo was delighted to get away from *Fantasy Island* kinds of stuff and do a really good movie. The character they promised they would write for him was absolutely fabulous. And they did.

The single most controversial aspect of the film was Spock

dying. Gene objected to that rather strenuously. Also, of all things, he objected to the playing of bagpipes at the funeral. Gene didn't care for that, even though he was well in with the Los Angeles Police Department, and the LAPD had their own pipe band.

Harve called me up about it. I don't know why he called me specifically; maybe because, on the one hand, I would be the one playing the bagpipes and he wanted to feel me out on it, or, on the other, I had a long-standing relationship with Gene. Harve told me what he wanted to do, and I said, "It sounds okay to me."

"Gene doesn't like it," he said.

I told him, "Who's the boss? Are you the boss?"

"Yeah."

"Then you have to do what you have to do," I said.

But, I'll tell you, I know that Harve was in charge, but I felt he cut my part in the film to shreds. It amounted to perhaps five minutes of the film, highlighting my relationship with my young nephew, Peter Preston. It set up the strong feeling of affection that Scotty had for the lad. It set up Scotty's hauling Preston's fried body up to sick bay, his stricken attitude when Preston died. In short, it explained material that had been left in the film. In a story as strong as *Wrath of Khan,* why have *any* sequences that are going to leave the viewers scratching their heads in confusion for any reason? I know the impetus is to make films as short as possible so theaters can have more showings in the course of a day. But would it really have killed them to make the film five minutes longer?

I wish Harve Bennett could have been standing next to me at conventions as puzzled fans asked me what was going on with Scotty in that film. Not to mention that the scene where Peter Preston dies was a damned good emotional scene that was just cut to pieces.

But Nick, who is a gem, put it all back when ABC aired the movie. Nick had been very appreciative, very complimentary of my work, particularly in those scenes. I gave him what he wanted, and Harve edited it out. But Nicholas Meyer restored it all.

Wrath was more or less the last chance for the movie series, and it performed beyond anyone's expectations. From the moment of the film's initial success, word began circulating about the next film. You have to understand something about the *Star Trek* movie rumor mill: It's constant. Walter, in particular, is tapped into every single possible rumor that floats through fandom, if not Hollywood. The question isn't so much when did I hear about the next film or the next or the next, but when *didn't* I hear about it. There was never a lack of rumors. So that when a particular offer did come through for the next film, it was hardly what anyone would call a surprise.

Star Trek III: The Search for Spock was Leonard's directing debut. Leonard is a good director, the best one we ever had when you get right down to it. Leonard was not the writer that Nicholas Meyer was, but he was a much better director. Leonard was prepared for everything; he knew exactly how the scene was going to be staged, and he staged it. He worked it out the night before. He didn't put up with any gobbledygook that anyone else might start to give him. Nor would he be swayed by Bill's usual tactic of "taking the director aside" and lobbying for a scene to be staged in a way that was advantageous to him.

But, I don't think the story in *Star Trek III* was good enough. There's not enough action in it—not to mention the fact that it was the first one where Leonard, as Spock, was absent almost the entire film. There was just something about the removal of the Vulcan from the mix that took some wind out of the sails.

Star Trek IV: The Voyage Home was a fabulous idea, a big whoop-de-do about saving the whales. The Greenpeace people loved it, and all the environmentalists absolutely adored it. That doesn't surprise me, because it was a beautiful story. One of my favorite moments is when we've landed the invisible Klingon vessel in the middle of a park, and Bill says, "Everybody remember where we parked." In retrospect, it shouldn't have been too hard to find; just look for the area of grass with the big imprint from the landing struts.

But, in my opinion, the best scene in the whole thing was the scene with Bill, Leonard, and Catherine Hicks in the truck, talking about where they're going to eat. Beautiful, beautiful scene.

I have to tell you about Catherine Hicks. Catherine was a sweet girl and a good little actress, but she pretended that she didn't know anything about acting. Heck, who knows, maybe she didn't.

We were at the point in the story where the Klingon ship has crashed into the water. We're in the engine room with the whales, she and I can't get out, we're sopping, and if the ship sinks any more we're drowned. We're dead. Captain Kirk is supposed to come and help us out.

Before the shot, Catherine says to me, "What should we be thinking right now?"

I stared at her as if she'd sprouted a third eye. "Survival," I said reasonably. Honestly, what else? Obviously we were in a situation where we were going to either live or die, and living seemed the preferred option.

She said, "Oh." But that didn't deter her from asking other questions about acting, all the time.

We also had a sequence where we're perched outside the ship, with tons of water being poured on us, while standing in front of a blue screen. We started out with ninety-two degree weather, so we were lucky to be in the water. But eventually we found ourselves faced with seventy-eight degrees, which may sound sufficiently balmy, but with the fans going and water being shot at us at forty or fifty miles an hour, it was like stinging needles.

Still, that was very exciting to watch being filmed. As a

matter of fact, secretaries who hadn't been at Paramount very long would walk by and say, "Oh! Real movie making!" It was a terribly exciting part.

There was an outtake from that scene that got into the trailer for *Star Trek IV.* During one of the times when we were standing on the side of the ship, I slipped and fell into the water. What got into the movie was a take where I didn't slip, but fans are so sharp-eyed that they noticed it and asked about it.

At a convention in Springfield, Massachusetts, a young boy asked, "Can you transport things that are moving?"

I remembered that whenever we had to be transported, we were all standing perfectly still. So I answered, "No, you can't."

Then, five minutes later, an even younger boy—or a very young looking midget—said, "Well, sir, if you can't transport things that are moving, how did you move the whales in *Star Trek IV?"*

I ended up saying, "We caught them at a frozen moment," whatever that meant. That didn't even begin to account for the water the whales were in, which was also moving. I looked at the audience and said, "Boy, out of the mouths of babes . . ."

Those were the sharpest questions I'd ever had from anybody, and they came from a bunch of kids. Of course, the parents may have coaxed them into it. I tell that joke now before I start into my question-and-answer sessions, because I don't want parents to send their "brilliant brats" to sandbag me.

Yes, I've since realized that the transporters have been "updated" in the movies so that people *can* be in motion while transporting—such as when Kirk and Saavik were conversing while transporting in *The Wrath of Khan.* So don't try and catch me with that one again, because I'm ready for you!

While we were busy filming *Star Trek IV,* there wasn't any

need to speculate about whether or not there would be another film. Bill made it clear that not only was one in the hopper, but he was writing it. He said, "I'm writing a script for the next movie, and we're going to show you what your characters really are." As you might imagine, that pronouncement made it a bit more difficult to focus on what was going on in *The Voyage Home.* None of us were exactly breathless with anticipation over the next film.

There was a scene in *The Voyage Home* wherein I endeavor to operate a twentieth-century computer. When it fails to respond to voice command, I'm handed a mouse and promptly start to speak into it. I had a lot of fun with that scene. It had a sort of Laurel and Hardy sensibility to it. I always looked upon DeForest as Ollie and I was Stanley.

It was a motif that kept going beyond the film. DeForest, Nichelle, George, Walter, and I shot our last scenes—the heads for the time travel sequence. Those people should sell those heads because those were great, and they really looked like us. I'd pay three thousand or four thousand dollars for something like that.

We finished at about ten-fifteen in the morning, and we were scheduled to be transported back at four-thirty from Monterey to Los Angeles, connecting through San Francisco. So we got after them and said, "C'mon, let's get out of here.

After about half an hour, we got into an airplane, a prop plane, and we sat there and sat there, and nobody told us why. The air conditioner came on and produced a hum. I said, in a Stan Laurel–voice, "Ollie?"

De turned around and said, "Yes?"

"Ollie, I wonder if we should tell the pilot that a hum isn't going to get us there." The whole place broke up (except for one person who obviously didn't understand the whole thing—I guess).

That started a whole string of jokes; we were doing shtick back and forth, and hilarity continued throughout the trip. We got to San Francisco very late, tried to get a flight out from there, got into a plane that moved away from the terminal . . . and then moved back because they were fixing a runway.

Nichelle took George, whom she was sitting beside, out to the airport bar. While they were there, the doors were suddenly closed and the plane pulled away from the terminal. We took off without George and Nichelle. Well, we just knew what Nichelle would be thinking when she got back, that she was not being treated properly and everything else. Poor George would bear the brunt of the whole thing.

We finally got down to Los Angeles, and I said to Walter, "Let's get a limo," because Paramount hadn't bothered to provide us with transportation. Which is what we did . . . except that Nichelle apparently heard about it and didn't realize that we had commissioned the limo ourselves. She called me up and said, "You took my limo!"

I said, "What the hell are you talking about? There were no limousines waiting, none at all!"

She said, "Oh." And that was that, but, God, what a day.

So there I was on the set of *Star Trek V: The Final Frontier,* a corridor set that had cost $190,000. Bill's boast about this movie during the filming of *The Voyage Home* was still ringing in my ears, and I was faced with it now.

Apparently what he intended to prove was that Mr. Scott's greatest boast about his alleged mastery of the *Enterprise* was so much hot air. Because this scene called for me to swagger down the corridor, boasting, "I know this ship like the back of my hand," smash my head into an overhead beam, and be knocked unconscious.

And "One-Take" Doohan was heading into his fortieth take on that one scene.

Not that I hit my head forty times. But we were walking down that corridor and I couldn't even get the lines out. The set had been built just for that laugh. Now, I'm an actor, I'm supposed to do a job, and that's what I was going to do. But I found that very, very hard to do because I felt—whether it was Bill's intention or not—that he had constructed the scene just to put me down.

No one was particularly enthused about being directed by Bill. I saw and heard Leonard and De snickering when they were off by themselves, waiting for him to make some new mistake. So it's not as if I was the only one.

I'll tell you, the fans went into a bloody uproar about that head-bump gag. It got a knee-jerk laugh because it was unexpected, but it was humor that was derived at the expense of the character. Because when Scotty says, "I know this ship like the back of my hand," that's not a setup line for a gag. He really *does* know it that well. The fans didn't like it. They'd say things to me like, "I hated that scene. Why did you dare to do it? Why didn't you object to that?"

And I'd say, "Hey, they paid one hundred and ninety thousand dollars for that set alone."

If you look at that moment in the film, you can see how tired I am after forty takes. And in between them, Bill was just standing there, patient as hell. But, boy, I'm telling you, I'd never want to have Bill write and direct another film of mine. That's for sure.

That script also revealed the previously totally unknown romantic attraction between Scotty and Uhura. I don't know what Nichelle thought about it, but I thought the same thing Scotty did. Personally, I really love Nichelle. I think she's just a fabulous lady. But I don't think, all of a sudden, out of nowhere, we should become lovers. I think Scotty's reaction to it was exactly what Jimmy Doohan's would be—a kind of slack-jawed, "Huh? Where did *that* come from?" It certainly wasn't set up.

I didn't like the final product. Even Gene had tried to warn Bill off from the subject matter, saying, "Come on . . . nobody depicts God." The fight was going to be between Kirk and God . . . and Kirk wins! Come on! Gene told him, "Hey, come on, you cannot do that. Nobody does that."

This was the last film that Gene lived to see to completion. I think that Gene, in the last years of the movies, was very, very happy with the movies (his objections to Bill's premise notwithstanding).

The *Star Trek* franchise took a serious hit with the less-than-enthusiastic reception of *The Final Frontier.* And as happened once before when the franchise was foundering, Nicholas Meyer came riding in to save the day. This came as a great relief to all of us, since they might have had trouble talking the cast into participating if Bill had been helming the film once more.

To me, *Star Trek VI: The Undiscovered Country* is our best. Directed and cowritten by Nick Meyer, it was one hell of a film.

As I mentioned earlier, I thought that *Star Trek* was at its best when it told stories that had a relation to the real world, that commented on actual elements of our society.

Nothing could have been more topical, more powerful, or more meaty for one of our films than a story that related to the fall of the Soviet Union. On that basis—considering the groundwork laid for the Federation/Klingon alliance, and the tapestry that it played against—*The Undiscovered Country* was our most ambitious endeavor. And here was the kicker: The script was written long before the Soviet Union dissolved. Talk about a story with an eye toward the future.

I was down being measured for a uniform for *Star Trek VI,* and Nicholas came down to wardrobe and said, "I hear you're signed, and that's why you're here." And he came up and hugged me.

Still, there was one time when he let us down. We were scheduled to shoot the scene where Valeris (Kim Catrell) is revealed to be a traitor, and she's going to be questioned on the bridge. Nicholas had not mentally staged the scene the night before. He came in unprepared. Bill wanted to do it one way, and Nicholas wasn't sure.

And as it happened, I said, "Why don't you put her down

there on the floor alone and everybody else, her judges, up on the deck behind the captain's chair. That solves the problem." That's how they wound up staging it, and Bill looked astounded that I had come up with that.

Also, there was something Walter told me about. During the rehearsals for the final scene—as the crew was preparing to sail off "until morning"—Walter did a certain expression and Bill said, "C'mon, don't do that, don't make that face."

Walter said, "Well, okay."

Although, I'll tell you, Bill may have talked Walter out of reacting in a certain way, but I thought the expression on Bill's face in that final scene was a *lot* like the way Walter had been playing it.

I figured after *The Undiscovered Country* that that was pretty much it. The character of Mr. Scott was effectively retired. So imagine my surprise when I was tapped for an episode of *Star Trek: The Next Generation* entitled "Relics."

I admit, when *Star Trek: The Next Generation* was announced, I was among the cast members who voiced displeasure or anger or annoyance. I watched four of the first shows, and they were just doing our shows. I didn't like that part. I said to Gene, "What's the matter, don't you have any writers?" And he foofarawed and harrumphed an awful lot. I didn't watch for quite a long while after that. Then my children started watching, and they called me in. And I said, "Oh, *The Next Generation,* eh?" And I watched fifteen, twenty minutes of it, then through to the end, and you know, it wasn't bad.

I know I was the first of the original cast members to go back on the idea that *The Next Generation* was an insult to the original cast. I took Gene to lunch one day and said, "Gene, I just wanted to say I know damn well how hard it is to produce a new series. I just wanted to let you know that I'm not going to publicly say one word about it after this." Hell, I even went on *Win, Lose or Draw* with Michael Dorn.

I was pleased when they decided to revive Scotty for *The*

Next Generation, particularly since they were doing it in a way that avoided my having to endure three hours of aging makeup. Pulling me out of a sort of transporter suspended animation made the return of Scotty a much more alluring proposition.

The only thing I didn't like was all the technical terms. I had scenes where I was talking with LeVar Burton and we were tossing around technobabble fast and furious. I talked to Michael Pillar about that after the fact, and I said, "That's just too much. That's not the way engineers would talk to each other. I mean, engineers would know the thing and say it. In other words, instead of saying, 'I want you to figure that trickus,' they'd say, 'I'll tell you what, you join those two together and that should be all right.' That's the way they'd be talking together about this big technical thing."

Compare *The Next Generation* to original *Star Trek* sometime. Let's say the engines are in trouble. Geordi will say, "If I can reroute the isometric ion pulse through the engine core, then maybe I can temporarily backload the matter-antimatter resonance." Scotty would say, "Ah'm holdin' 'em together with spit and bailing wire, Captain, but it won't last for long."

But Michael Pillar told me, "Well, Rick Berman likes it." And I said, "Well, geez, y'know, he's the boss. And he's this great guy. But the point is, I wish he wouldn't be so technical because it's just not done. Engineers talk plainly to each other. They don't show their expertise by using every damned word in the dictionary.

I needed cue cards to handle all the jargon. I had to have them, and I never had to work off cue cards before that I can recall. I really grew to admire LeVar Burton for being able to spout that stuff. But then, he's a heck of a lot younger than I am. When I was younger, I could do it, too.

The cast treated me like a king. If they had all been Japanese, they'd have been bowing in front of me. That's exactly how they treated me, with the absolute greatest deference. It was absolutely fantastic. They were all, to me, damned good actors, and I loved them.

Patrick Stewart particularly was just fabulous, as was Marina Sirtis. LeVar Burton was really just a terrific guy. I understand he studied for the priesthood at first. That's kind of a shock somehow.

Gates McFadden was terrific, and was so apologetic when she came back and asked for some autographs. "Could I get some please?" she asked. God, I'd have given her anything. She was terrific, so was Jonathan Frakes and Michael Dorn.

Brent Spiner was great to work with. As I mentioned earlier, we had that wonderful twist on the scene from "By Any Other Name," with Data holding up a bottle of liquor and saying, "It is green."

And when that episode was over, I figured, Okay, that's it. That's finally paid, finished, over and out, for Scotty.

I should've known better. . . .

Several cast members said they didn't want to be in *Star Trek Generations,* the feature film. I think I was not in the original script that they wrote. Just Spock, McCoy, and Kirk were. That was the version that I saw.

But obviously, what's Leonard going to do there when he's only got five lines. Leonard doesn't need the money because he's already made millions in a couple of movies. What a hell of a pension that is. DeForest was in the same position, with a handful of lines and no driving financial need to make it since he's got nobody to look after but his wife. He's paid his mortgage. He probably got close to a million for the last movie anyway. So, obviously, with only a few lines, they said, "To hell with it."

Now, me, I knew very well I would increase my income significantly by being in the movie. I was building a new house and everything else. I wanted to make as much money as I could, mostly for my wife. So, to hell with it. I figured I would take whatever money I could get, so long as it didn't take me too long to get it.

I'd gotten a new agent some fifteen years ago, a great guy named Steve Stevens. Six years ago, I even brought George over to the agency after George's agent passed away. I said, "You should come and talk to Steve."

Another client I eventually brought over to Steve was Walter Koenig. Although I brought Walter over to Steve for a time, Walter then left and went to some other agent. That other agent kept calling up Steve and saying, "What should I do?" On *Generations,* Walter called me up and asked me what I was getting for the movie.

I said, "Walter, this is private stuff! You call up Steve, and he's not going to tell you."

"Jimmy, it's my livelihood!" he said. Why didn't he trust his agent to get him what he's entitled to?

I was somewhat annoyed, but I finally told him what I was getting. I don't know what he got, because he never came around and told me.

In *Star Trek Generations,* we did a whole scene (eventually cut completely from the film) set in a wheat field, with me delivering opening lines about Kirk as he parachuted into the field. We did all that, and then I forgot it. Late in the afternoon, the director, David Carson, wanted to film some additional coverage on the scene. So he said, "Would you say those lines again?"

And I said, "David, we already shot that scene."

"You mean you've forgotten it already?" he said.

"Yeah. Shakespeare I never forget . . . but that was this morning! I'm not alive for those lines anymore."

"Well, will you try?" he asked.

I told him okay, and I redid the scene. But when I'm finished with a job, that's it. I don't want to go back and redo it.

When people come up to me and say, "Oh, you were marvelous in *Star Trek Generations,*" they're always referring to the same moment: the look on my face when Kirk is gone. I say hardly anything. Four or five guys who saw the dailies said, "Jimmy, you're just marvelous." I love to hear that.

That look . . . that astonished look of loss and tragedy . . . was the last official appearance of Montgomery Scott.

There was, however, one sort of "unofficial" appearance since then. Last year I went to New York City to work with Yakov Smirnoff on one of the hardest projects I've ever done.

I'm sure you're familiar with the wild rides at Disney parks with the big screens—*Star Tours,* for example—where your senses are tricked into thinking that you're on a high-speed ride while your seat tilts just enough to sell the illusion.

Well, they installed a new feature at the Empire State Building, a movie with Yakov and myself, and it's that same sort of ride—a "skytour" of New York City. Although my character is not officially Scotty, I certainly played it that way.

The audience enters a room, sidling into rows of seats, and then watches a film that—combined with seat movement— plays havoc with your sense of perspective. In the film you come off the top of the Empire State Building, then go downtown and in between the towers, narrowly avoid collisions . . . It's a wild ride. I play the pilot (with Scots burr, of course), and Yakov is a New York cabbie who somehow stumbled into my cockpit.

We had lines of dialogue, of course, and things would be happening to us that we had to react to. We'd be all over the place, shifting around. They would show us the film, then we would go into the cockpit and time the whole performance to the film.

There's a possibility that it'll also be shown in Paris, the Sears Tower in Chicago, and Tokyo.

The thing I don't quite understand is that Yakov had a guy there who was like his manager, but the guy was sometimes actually physically moving him around. He'd be saying, "No, no, do it this way. No, the line would be better so-and-so." Sometimes he'd try and change *my* lines. I never found out who the guy was.

There have been other cameos of Scotty—footage shot for the stage musical "Return to the Forbidden Planet," appearances on commercials and such.

It's amazing how involved the rest of the world became in Montgomery Scott, considering how close he was to me.

It's ironic, and sometimes I wonder if Scotty even counts as part of the twenty-year journey as an actor. Because with Scotty, so much of what made him unique came not from any great acting challenge, but instead were simply elements of James Doohan, and an accent. Scotty's a contradiction to the times when I've told people that, in the creation of a character, if you haven't lost one night's sleep, then you're not really working hard enough. Yet I worked about two seconds in the creation of Scotty. Anytime I do an accent, I know exactly whom I'm playing. Even in "Relics," I didn't do anything differently from what I did when I'd first incarnated the character thirty years ago. To me, Scotty is Scotty and was already a full human being as soon as I opened my mouth with a Scottish accent.

I tell people that he's one percent accent and ninety-nine percent James Doohan. Although that might be oversimplifying it. The way I look at Scotty is, hey, I love engineering myself. I wish I could be an engineer. Scotty may not be so much James Doohan as he is an idealized version of James Doohan. A James Doohan who, as a boy, loved things that "went" and dreamed of escape.

Indeed, how much further can you escape than the stars?

18

One Trek Beyond

I WASN'T ENTHUSED ABOUT THE PROSPECT OF DOING A SOAP OPERA. They only paid a thousand dollars an episode, they weren't going to fly me in, and they didn't pay for hotel. But Steve Stevens, my agent, was extremely persuasive, and the next thing I knew, I was heading out to appear in *The Bold and the Beautiful.*

And—try not to be shocked—I was to play a Scotsman. Figured. After twenty-five years with the image of me tossing about a Scots burr, what else what they going to cast me as?

But not just any Scotsman, mind you. I was an angry, dirty, alcoholic, damned old father.

So there I was, finishing out the end of my four-week, eleven episode commitment. I was on the second to last scene, a final confrontation with my son, our entire lifetime of antagonism and antipathy brought to a head. Present also was the woman who loved him, who reamed me out and told me what a bastard I was—how I'd nearly destroyed my son's life.

But the son was gentle with me, understanding of my frailties, forgiving of the hurt and anguish that I'd caused him. In short, he was everything that I hadn't been with my own father on that day so long ago, when I'd seen him for the last time.

With the cameras rolling, I reached for a drink of scotch. The subtext of the scene was clear: without saying anything, I was pleading for my son to forgive me. He put his hand on my arm before I could down the scotch and said, "C'mon, now, Dad, you don't need that anymore."

I looked up at him, and he said, "I forgive you, dad."

It was all turned around. There I was, portraying the embittered, angry alcoholic whose actions had haunted his son's life.

Once upon a time, I had been unable to generate tears as an actor. Once upon a time, I had had the same confrontation with my father, seen from the other side through the hurt eyes of an angry young man. Once upon a time, I had been unable to find it within me to extend forgiveness to the man I was now portraying.

And the tears just burst out of my eyes, pouring down my face. I jumped up from my seat, hugging my "son" as the tears welled up. Twenty seconds of sobbing passed before the director yelled, "Cut."

There was a long pause in the control room upstairs. After about five or six minutes, they said, "Can we see that again?" And you know what? I did it again . . . only this time it was better.

Then another long while went by, and I know damn well that this time they had called up the supervising producer and told him, "Get down here." I'm sure that's what happened, because they said, "Can we see that again?" And I said, "Fine, sure," and everybody else said okay.

But the girl that I was looking at, the one who was telling me what a bastard I had been . . . now *she* had tears in her eyes. They don't normally do that.

It was all in the lessons that Sandy Meisner had first drilled into me—the concept of doing things under imaginary circumstances. Or the example, which Meisner gave, of Eleonora Duse, a famous Italian actress, who would write comments on the sides of her script such as, "Oh, that poor girl! Look at what's happening to her! Why is she doing this to me!"

The twenty-year journey, disrupted, detoured, and extended, but coming to a conclusion nonetheless . . . in part due to a real-life scene being played out to a different conclusion, an alternate and heightened reality that my father once held in such disdain.

And best of all, I got a rave review from not only the people on hand and the executive producer, but *TV Guide.* It's nice to get that kind of recognition after all this time. A validation that even *he* might have approved of.

So let's reverse our opening scenario.

The younger version of me is on the set of *Star Trek,* the ink still drying on his newly signed contract. He looks at me, his future self. He knows who I am, where I came from, knows that I know the future. And with some slight trepidation, he asks:

"If you had it to do over again . . . would you?"

I think about the kind of career I've had. The things I haven't done and would like to do and don't know if I'll ever be able to.

There are acting challenges I'd still like to take on, people I'd still like to work with—Michael Douglas, for example. I like the Bridges boys, Beau and Jeff, and their father, Lloyd. I love Elisabeth Shue, a very talented girl. I like Susan Sarandon, Sally Field.

In terms of roles I'd like to play, at least fifteen people have told me that I should play Falstaff. I'd love to play King Lear. I was in a production of *King Lear* in Toronto, playing the earl of Kent, a character who is a great friend of Lear's. But Lear himself is a symphony; it's not the greatest audience pleaser in the world, but audiences love to see all sorts of people play Lear because that's a big test of an actor.

But when you consider Mr. Scott, and you consider the

impact that he and *Star Trek* have had, it makes me realize that it goes far beyond the simple concerns of an acting career.

I've been to an awful lot of research labs and they're delighted to have me . . . if for no other reason than that I'm Mr. Scott. I've been to Cape Canaveral for three blastoffs. I get absolutely red-carpet treatment. I've got video on that to show how I'm treated. They show me everything. I've seen the *Columbia* flat on its belly, twenty feet off the floor, while they looked for a hydrogen leak. They put the uniform on me and taped my mustache, covered my hair, and I climbed up into the cargo bay.

I worked the robot arm, which is made in Canada. I went to the vehicle assembly building and saw the *Discovery* in there, on its launch pad, and the big tractor that will move it. They were loading solid rocket propellant into it. It's all loaded on and connected up before they move it onto the pad.

I'm just thrilled to see that, and thrilled that I'm Scotty and can get in to see those things.

There was an Air Force general who was in charge of the *Atlantis* on the pad, and we had to ask permission to see it. He said, "Scotty? Sure, you let him come in."

I have an honorary doctorate in engineering, given to me by the Milwaukee School of Engineering (established in 1903). Fifty percent of their students respond to the question, "Why would you like to be an engineer?" with, "Because I'd like to follow Scotty" or "Scotty was my inspiration for getting into it."

I've been to China Lake five times. A good friend of mine, Ron Derr, is the civilian in charge. There's a scientist there who works with little computer chips, and he told me that shortly after the year 2000 they'll be able to put one of those in the back of your skull, connect it to your brain, and on that chip will be everything known in the world. You'll just have to press a little button to activate it and know everything there is to know. This is what he's thinking about.

I've been inspired by Scotty myself to read technical journals. I can't do the formulas and some of the things I don't understand, but a great majority of it I do understand.

I've been to labs all over the country. I've been to Hughes Research in Malibu, and I've been to Louis Research Center, at the airport in Cleveland, a couple of times. One of the scientists, in response to a question I asked, looked at me as if to say, "Boy, you're way ahead of us, way ahead of what we were planning to tell you."

I've seen all the different plans for building space platforms—some of them are just plain extension things that go up in a rocket and are pulled out to become a rigid piece of steel. It thrills me to see that stuff.

And the only way I would ever have gotten to those places is because I'm Scotty.

Scotty came about because I used to do imitations of other people. Now people do imitations of me as Scotty. I heard about one fan production that had "Scotty" teaching a group of cadets, pointing to a blackboard and saying, "Okay, lads . . . repeat after me." And he indicated the following sentence: "Captain, the engines canna take it ennymore." And every cadet intoned, in a scots burr, "Captain, the engines canna take it ennymore."

The best Scotty imitator, though, was Jay Leno, who was imitating me years and years before he was a big star. He was the best one.

Would I do it again?

If it weren't for Mr. Scott, I would never have met Wende. Nor would we have had two sons, Eric and Tom, both in their late teens. Tom, inventive and interested in music, and Eric, the literatus of the family, an aspiring actor and a hell of a writer. When he was thirteen, he wrote a twenty-seven-page story that was so beautiful I said to Wende, "We've got a Hemingway on our hands."

And Tom, what a great kid. Once, some years ago, Wende's father had been visiting us. I'm in the unusual circumstance of being older than my father-in-law. I was driving Thomas to bowling, and he said, "You know . . . you're older than Grandpa, but you've got more spunk."

The time-portal effect starts to crackle around me, to take me back to Seattle, to Wende and Eric and Tom and our newly built home. My younger version still looks apprehensive, not sure if he's thrilled with the prospect of being in his seventies and faced with regrets about parts he would have liked to play. He shouts after me as the future pulls me back, *"Are you happy?"*

Am I happy?

I think I am. Despite all the typecasting, the missed parts, I am basically a happy person. I am happy, particularly now, because *Star Trek* is going away and I'm going back to getting rave reviews again, which I used to get before *Star Trek.*

So, to me, I am mostly happy with my work. I know what I'm doing. If you know what you're doing, there's no doubt about it that if you get the right part, you'll get rave reviews. To me, that's the essence. I am happy doing my work. And I wish I could do a lot more work.

To tell you the honest truth, I guess I do regret not having played all those other characters I know I would have played. But to do that, I would have to stop being Scotty. I'd lose the negatives . . . but the positives, as well.

If *Star Trek* had not come along, I think my life as an actor would be just as good as it is now. I really think it would be just as good, because over the past thirty years I would have gotten a lot of other parts that people would now know me for. I would have the reputation of being an actor, whereas now I have the reputation of being Scotty.

But under no circumstance would I want to be without Wende, Eric, and Tom.

I know the effect that *Star Trek*—and, by extension, I— have had on people's lives. I see it every time I do a convention. I see it in the faces of people at the stores.

To some people, the crew of the *Starship Enterprise* have

achieved the status of legends. I sure don't feel like a legend, although sometimes I feel I had better try to live up to that status.

I believe I'm getting my just desserts through my work, and part of my work is Scotty, y'know? I think possibly, if I live long enough, I will get some of those other roles where people can see the acting. And they'll say, "Geez . . . I didn't know he could do that. Isn't that amazing?"

And people will say, "Well, he practiced an awful lot on *Star Trek,* I guess."

ACKNOWLEDGMENTS

Skip this part. Skip right over it. Under no circumstance should you be aware that there are folks whose involvement on this book was critical and should be acknowledged to all and sundry.

(Boy, I hope reverse psychology works.)

First and foremost, my wife, the intrepid Myra David. While I was out of the country involved in a lengthy television project, she provided invaluable aid by sifting through hundreds of pages of my transcribed conversations with Jimmy Doohan. Conversations which had strayed all over the place, moving through all moments of his life with almost reckless abandon. Myra cross-referenced it, organizing it by subject matter. In short, she provided me with what turned out to be an absolutely essential index so that I could then hammer the manuscript into chronological order. Simply put, I could not have done it without her. Then again, as I look back on the last twenty years of my life, I can think of nothing of consequence I've ever accomplished that I *could* have done without her. (She also suggested the title for the book which we didn't use: *Doohan Time*. Sure, the final title is more "Trek friendly," but darn, I liked her idea.)

I should also mention my daughters, Ariel and Gwen (who understand what "Daddy's on deadline" means) and, particularly in this instance, Shana, who was present during some of the interviews, was utterly charming, and also had a great time hanging out with Jimmy's wife. She was pleasant company to have during some very interesting times.

I must also thank Pat O'Neill, contributing editor to *Wizard* magazine and long time friend. Pat undertook the herculean task of doing all the transcribing, fitting it in between his job requirements and the needs of his sons, Brian and Timmy, and his patient wife, Jill. Pat stepped in to handle the job since I didn't trust outside transcription agencies to do it (since details of other biographies seem to have a habit of leaking prior to publication.) I needed someone who could handle the assignment and could be trusted to keep the contents of the transcripts to himself. Well done, Pat.

I'd like to thank Kevin Ryan, long-time friend and Pocket Books editor who first tagged me for this assignment, giving me something new and different to put on my resume, as well as Margaret Clark who stepped in and handled the transition smoothly when Kevin went on to move to more purple pastures. I'd also like to thank George Takei, accomplished autobiographer (to say nothing of fearsome warlord) whose advice at several key points was extremely helpful.

There's also Bobbie Chase, Kevin Dooley, Chris Duffy, Joey Cavalieri, Richard Howell, and others of my long suffering editors at Marvel, DC and Claypool Comics who cut me slack time on my other projects while I worked on this one.

ACKNOWLEDGMENTS

And last—but not least—James and Wende Doohan, whose graciousness, hospitality and frankness made this one of the most stimulating and involving projects with which I've ever been associated. My thanks to them and to all of you who didn't skip this part.

Peter David
New York and Montreal
July 1996